STOP
—THE—
SHOW!

A History of Insane Incidents  *er*

Brad Schreiber

THUNDER'S MOUTH PRESS
NEW YORK

STOP THE SHOW!: *A History of Insane Incidents and Absurd Accidents in the Theater*

Published by
Thunder's Mouth Press
An Imprint of Avalon Publishing Group, Inc.
245 West 17th Street, 11th floor
New York, NY 10011

AVALON
publishing group incorporated

Library of Congress Cataloging-in-Publication Data is available.

ISBN-10: 1-56025-820-9
ISBN-13: 978-1-56025-820-9

Book design by Maria E. Torres

Printed in the United States of America
Distributed by Publishers Group West

With love to Andrew Schreiber, PhD, aka Dad, whose strength, compassion, and courage shall always inspire me

CONTENTS

PREFACE

THE INSPIRATION FOR this book, oddly enough, was Cyril Clayton's private parts.

In the mid-1980s, Cyril was performing a role in Terrence McNally's play *Noon* in San Francisco. A friend and I went to support Cyril as audience members.

In this farce, Cyril was playing a middle-aged man who's into sadomasochistic sex. He wore a frighteningly small leather bikini brief, held up by leather straps and studded with metal. He looked like he was wearing Nazi S&M lederhosen.

Cyril is a round, balding, boisterous, charming Englishman. I am convinced he would have been a successful music hall comedian in a previous lifetime. He more than makes up for the lack of hair on his head with the hair on his chest, stomach, legs, shoulders, ears, and other areas you generally don't need it.

Cyril got plenty of laughs that night with his outfit and personality. But what really brought down the house was this: while he was running about onstage, one of his testicles popped out of his kinky leather underwear and swung about like a chandelier at a wild party.

The audience laughed loudly. Cyril, God love him, thought it was due to his broad characterization and redoubled his efforts to jump around onstage. The more his scrotum danced about, the more the audience roared.

My friend and I laughed until we could not breathe, but all the while, we were horrified. This was our friend, being utterly humiliated without even knowing it. The audience was "having a ball" at his expense.

I told other theater artists about the Cyril story, emphasizing its peculiar blend of horror and hilarity. What I found fascinating was that these other directors, actors, playwrights, technicians, and designers often had this kind of response: "Oh, yeah, hanging out of his underwear. Listen, I have a *really* good story . . ." And often, they did.

Theater is like no other performing art. It is live human beings in real time. There can be no editing out of mistakes. If you're injured, you carry on. If you forget your line, someone else onstage covers for you. Some twigs can be a forest. A beauty salon can double as a performance space.

Theater has no restrictions as to language or subject matter. And the written word is sacred. You say the writer's words as intended, no matter who you are, no matter how big a star. (Unless some scenery falls on you, in which case you are entitled to make up a line of your own.)

Is it any wonder, then, considering this most immediate of art forms, that one could become obsessed with finding the most mindboggling stories of things that took place during a live performance?

I have worked in the theater as a playwright, actor, director, and producer, and when I was in two comedy troupes, the Burlingame Philharmonic Orchestra and Friends of the Ozone, I even designed costumes, properties, and sound. As a theater critic, I've sat through many a play that made me cringe, that made me want to shriek and run out of the theater, frothing at the mouth.

So why do I still love it? Because when it works, my friends, when it really works, there is nothing like it. The emotions are deeper. The laughs are richer. It is more powerful than the most expensive special effects movie that will ever be made.

It is live humans in real time, subject to the laws of gravity, memory, and audience audacity.

And when something unplanned happens, whether it is handled superbly or horribly, it lives in your mind forever. It becomes its own very special, elevated form of theater.

—Brad Schreiber,
Los Angeles, February 2006

1

At a Loss for Words
(Actors' Lines)

JOHN GIELGUD WAS celebrating the centenary of Henrik Ibsen in the play *Ghosts* with Mrs. Patrick Campbell, and no doubt, the production probably felt like it lasted a hundred years, too. While Mrs. Campbell was renowned for her acting abilities, she was not recommended for her manners. She insulted the man playing Pastor Manders during one performance by turning her back to the audience and announcing, with a look of disgust on her face, "Oh, look at that old man with the sweat pouring onto his stomach."

That would have been more than enough, but during rehearsals for the same run, Campbell insisted on coaching the young Gielgud on a particular scene in which he would point to his forehead and, referring to a mental illness, say, "The disease I suffer from is seated here."

During their first performance, just before Gielgud recited this emotional line, which he and Campbell had practiced scores of times, she announced to him aside, lackadaisically, "Oh, I am so hungry."

Allowing an ensemble to improvise lines can be treacherous, especially if the background actors are a bit too creative.

When Michael Benthall was directing *Julius Caesar* at the Old Vic, he castigated the ensemble for a lack of authenticity in their background reactions. "Just behave as you would normally in a crowded street," he told them.

That night, a member of a crowd scene walked offstage in his toga, shouting "Taxi!"

Another production of *Julius Caesar* proved that when things go wrong onstage, one of the best ways to cover up the mess is to blame it all on a character who is dead.

Caesar was quite dead, both in real life and in the Shakespeare play, when Joseph Maher and John Tillinger (now a noted director) were performing at the American Shakespeare Festival in Stratford, Connecticut.

Maher and Tillinger had killed the emperor, but no one had bothered to kill the ringer on the pay phone, newly installed backstage.

With the dead body of Caesar bloody at their feet, the actors and audience heard the pay phone ring and ring.

Finally, Maher turned to Tillinger and asked conspiratorially, "What if it's for Caesar?"

Vedrenne-Eadie Management in London got their money's worth out of actress Gladys Cooper. She was onstage only in the last thirty minutes of Arnold Bennett and Edward Knoblock's *Milestones*. So she was systematically rented out for first acts and matinees.

One month, she was lent out to the Drury Lane theater, where she would "die" onstage as the character Beauty in *Everywoman*; then, after the show, she would dash across London in order to do her role in *Milestones*.

This exhausting schedule came back to bite everyone involved on the collective butt. When Cooper died one evening onstage as Beauty, she actually fell asleep on the stage. No one knew anything was wrong, since she was feigning death, until an actor left the stage and slammed the onstage door.

Cooper suddenly woke up and, forgetting where she was, shouted, "What the hell was that?"

The great Ralph Richardson wasn't feeling so great in a London drawing room comedy after World War II. He suddenly startled the actors and audience by asking that dreaded line, "Is there a doctor in the house?"

A man bravely stood up in the audience.

"How do you find the play, doctor?" asked Richardson. "Feeble, don't you think?"

Richard Pryor, one of the greatest comedians of our time, was still searching for his own style, performing mundane material, when singer Bobby Darin threw a Los Angeles party in his honor. It was there that another comedy legend, Groucho Marx, lovingly criticized him for his lack of risky material.

"Do you want a career you're proud of," Groucho demanded, "or do you want to end up a spitting wad like Jerry Lewis?"

Apparently, this intense interaction had a great deal to do with Pryor's renowned breakdown on stage at the Aladdin Hotel in Las Vegas in September 1967. Although Pryor referred to it as an "epiphany," the sold-out audience that night might not have been as charitable.

Pryor walked onto the stage, surveyed the audience, and asked that age-old burning question, "What the fuck am I doing here?" He walked offstage and, after that, his work began to dramatically improve.

Richard Newton was as noted for being a drunkard as he was for his acting. One afternoon, he was guzzling in a pub with fellow actor and professional drinker Wilfrid Lawson when he realized they had a matinee to perform.

They held each other up and stumbled to the theater, where they were scheduled to play in *Richard III*. Lawson lumbered onto the stage with his codpiece on backward, eliciting some laughter.

"If you think I'm pissed," Lawson warned those in the seats, "wait till you see the Duke of York!"

Orson Welles was not only large in talent and—in later years—in physical dimensions, he had a sizeable ego as well.

It was amply on display the night he planned to give a one-man show of Shakespearean readings in Phoenix, Arizona—and only five people showed up to see him.

Welles introduced the evening this way: "I am an actor, a writer, a director of both films and plays, an architect, a painter, a stage designer, a brilliant cook, an expert on the *corrida* (bullfights), a conjuror, a collector, a connoisseur, an enfant terrible, and an authority on modern art. How come there are so many of me and so few of you?"

He was also a "drama queen." He left the theater.

Perhaps it is better that Richard Brinsley Sheridan died before the revival of his play *The School for Scandal* at the Queen's Theatre in the English suburb of Hornchurch.

Lady Sneerwell is given the line, "The paragraphs, you say, Mr. Snake, were all inserted?"

There must have been sneers aplenty when the actress playing Sneerwell asked, "The snakes, you say, Mr. Paragraph, were all inserted?"

"Yes, Your Majesty," replied a stunned actor and, not waiting to find out where exactly the snakes were inserted, the management quickly dropped the curtain and the play started over from the beginning.

During the play *Winter Journey* at the St. James Theatre on Broadway, Michael Redgrave and Sam Wanamaker often had short passages in which they improvised lines. One night, three weeks into the run, something Redgrave said during one of these passages bothered Wanamaker.

After the show, Wanamaker confronted Redgrave. "You called me a kike," he accused him.

"When?"

"Tonight. Onstage."

Redgrave explained that he in fact had called Wanamaker a "tyke," which the noted British actor went on to explain was an old Yorkshire term, half insult, half endearment. Furthermore, Redgrave had been doing a New York accent for the role, which no doubt accounted for the mistake.

Wanamaker was not feeling conciliatory. "I've got three witnesses," he insisted.

Relying on another, much-loved British expression, Redgrave answered, "Why don't you stuff your three witnesses?"

This was not the only problem between the two.

Later on during the run, Wanamaker, in the second act, developed a bit of stage business for himself, scraping a chair's legs on the stage. This went on, night after night, until Redgrave could stand it no more. One night, when Wanamaker began his noisemaking, the British thespian grabbed the chair with both hands.

Magically, during the next few shows, there was no scraping. But it wasn't long before Wanamaker recommenced his annoying habit.

On that night, Redgrave, who'd believed the problem had disappeared for good, burst out, "Don't do that!"

"Why not?" replied the shocked Wanamaker, also veering from the script.

"Because," said Redgrave, with a distinct edge in his voice, "it goes right through my head."

Redgrave and Wanamaker did not talk to each other offstage for six months during their icy *Winter Journey.*

Most instances of "drying" or "going up on lines" involve forgetting a portion of dialogue.

On July 24, 1984, British actor Paul Greenwood was lucky he could remember any lines whatsoever.

The play was the ironically titled *The Happiest Days of Your Life* by John Dighton. Greenwood entered by placing a golfing bag on a table; when it slid off, it seemed to signal that he would eventually want to do the same.

A pencil he was to use for notes had no lead. A pen he found had no ink. Greenwood, already rattled, began rewriting lines as he said them.

In the second act, he began spouting lines meant for other actors. Finally, he turned to the audience and apologized, "I'm sorry. We'll have to stop because I'm talking nonsense up here. You see, there was no lead in my pencil."

One of his fellow actors retorted, "That has always been your problem," bringing the house down.

By act 3, Greenwood's version of his own lines was so far from the actual script, he stopped again and asked the audience, "Shall I start again?"

"Yes!" came the resounding reply.

Luckily for everyone involved, he did not dare.

It is very unlikely that an actor today would sign on, for any price, to play a lead role in the Passion plays that were popular in France in the fifteenth century. The depiction of the life, death, and resurrection of Jesus Christ began as shorter works in Europe. But by the time Arnoul Gréban, canon of the church of Le Mans, wrote a Passion play around 1450 that consisted of 35,000 verses, someone should have, with all due respect, shouted, "Stop the show."

Apparently, in those days, length equaled devoutness. Gréban, along with his brother Simon, a monk at St. Riquier, composed an enormous mystery on *The Acts of the Apostles*. It was 62,000 verses long. The real mystery is how anyone sat through the entire performance at Bourges. The show lasted forty days.

In some Passion plays, the actor who performed the role of Christ had to recite nearly 4,000 lines. The scene of the crucifixion had to last as long as it was estimated to take in history. It is written that in 1437, the curé Nicolle, playing Jesus in Metz, was actually about to die on the cross and had to be hastily revived so that the performance could continue.

He had better luck than another priest, Jehan de Missey, who at that same Passion play, in the role of Judas, paid dearly for his betrayal of Jesus. He remained hanging on his cross so long onstage that his heart stopped and he had to be cut down and carried away for burial.

A more recent Passion play was *The Christus*, staged annually at Boston's New England Life Hall in the 1960s. But Reverend Joseph

Kierce of nearby Dorchester, who wrote the work, saw one performance turn unintentionally sacrilegious.

It will not ruin the suspense to say that the final scene of the play is the crucifixion of Christ, a role played by Jay Johannson. He was tied onto a large cross; similarly affixed was the character Barabbas. Tony Alicata, who played the young Jesus in earlier scenes, religiously watched the ending each night. One evening, Alicata witnessed the elderly actor playing Barabbas open his mouth to deliver a final, powerful line before his death on the cross. In the process, his upper plate of false teeth flew out of his mouth, fell twelve feet to the stage floor, and splattered into many pieces, totally upstaging Jesus Christ.

Johannson/Jesus, in fact, regained the audience's attention, but in entirely the wrong way. He began laughing uncontrollably. And, as he did so, his cross shook. The curtain, mercifully, immediately came down.

It could well be the only Passion play ever to have had a comedic ending.

Ron Harris directed a production of *One Flew Over the Cuckoo's Nest* at The Playhouse at the Von Braun Center in Huntsville, Alabama. One performance is quite notable. It took three months to complete.

In Dale Wasserman's play, adapted from the book by Ken Kesey, Randle McMurphy is trying to get other patients in a psychiatric hospital to vote on what to watch on TV. Fred Bourgeois, playing McMurphy, was putting so much into his performance one night that he leaped into the air and came down hard in his cowboy boots, shattering a shinbone.

As it was nearly the end of the first act, Bourgeois, in great pain, gamely continued. Backstage at intermission, Bourgeois no longer had to hold in his response and he shouted in pain. Paramedics arrived, put an inflatable cast on his leg, and took him away.

Harris then addressed the audience, beginning his curtain speech: "We always tell our actors to 'break a leg.' In this case, one did." It was decided that, with no understudy and the lead gone, the rest of the performance and the run had to be canceled.

However, three months later, Harris reassembled virtually the entire cast, including the recently healed Bourgeois, and they returned to the same theater. Their first night back, they finished what they'd started, beginning with the second act of *Cuckoo's Nest*. Then the run continued.

It occurred to Harris and the cast that the three months between acts qualified as the longest intermission in the history of the theater. A letter was written and sent with documentation to the *Guinness Book of World Records*, asking to be included for the Longest Intermission. The editors wrote back, saying it was indeed a unique and interesting record . . . but not one anyone would think to break.

Daniel Day-Lewis was cast as the Melancholy Dane when *Hamlet* was mounted at the National Theatre in 1989. And before long, Day-Lewis would become the Mentally Unstable Dane onstage.

First, the critics were unkind. Then, Day-Lewis took three weeks off to promote the film *My Left Foot*, which featured his intense performance as a mentally handicapped man. When he returned to Hamlet, Day-Lewis found life to be imitating art: as Hamlet talked to the ghost of his father, so too did Day-Lewis communicate with his own dead father.

On September 5, about forty-five minutes into the Bard's work, Day-Lewis, overcome with emotion after seeing his own deceased father onstage, walked off into the wings and slumped to the floor in tears, halting the production. Three stagehands could not get him to return.

Day-Lewis was later quoted later as saying, "I had a very vivid, almost hallucinatory moment in which I was engaged in a conversation with my father . . . I had to leave the stage because I was an empty vessel. I had nothing in me, nothing to say, nothing to give."

When Allison Lowery Fuller attended the College of William and Mary in Williamsburg, Virginia, she was assistant wig and makeup designer for the Stephen Sondheim musical *Into the Woods*.

In a scene between the witch and Rapunzel that accords with the fairy tale, the witch is supposed to magically remove—not cut off—the cascading hair of Rapunzel, thus preventing the handsome prince from climbing up her hair to her room.

Fuller and the others on the crew puzzled over how to accomplish this onstage and finally devised a removable ponytail of false hair for the actress playing Rapunzel to wear. It attached to the wig on Rapunzel's head and could be easily removed if the witch held the rest of the wig in place.

During one performance, the witch wickedly yanked on the ponytail but forgot to put her other hand on the rest of the wig. As a result, she tore off all of Rapunzel's blond hair, revealing the actress's pinned-up real hair underneath.

The actress playing Rapunzel collapsed on the floor in a heap, pretending to cry, but really hiding her laughter.

The witch, left to solve the problem she had created, did so with great élan. She threw the wig angrily at Rapunzel and brought down the house in a storm of laughter by declaring, "Now the prince will never love you because he knows you're not a real blonde!"

Only a legend like John Barrymore could get away with inventing the lines for an entire scene during a major production of a play in London.

One of his most startlingly inventive exchanges, without relying on the tedious text itself, was in the farce *The Dictator* by Dick Davis. In it, Barrymore was supposed to enter as the wireless operator with a dispatch on two long sheets of paper. He was to present it to fellow actor Willie Collier, who would then "read aloud" the report, in the process informing the audience as to the basic plot of the play.

Inexplicably, Barrymore entered on opening night not with two long pieces of paper, but with a small piece torn off of a menu, about the size of a postage stamp.

Barrymore got one line verbatim. "Here, chief, is the dispatch."

Collier looked, horrified, at the tiny piece of paper, realizing that in no way could he pretend to read a communication that would detail the basic elements of the plot on a piece of paper the size of his thumbnail.

He improvised, "But where is the dispatch? The real one?"

That was Collier's crucial error. He invited Barrymore to make up the rest of the scene with him.

"Here it is, sir," Barrymore parried, getting a little more aggressive. "Or have your eyes gone back on you again?"

"Go to the wireless room," ordered Collier, "and bring the first dispatch. There are two sheets of it. Remember? That's the one I want to read. Not a piece of confetti."

"But this is the first dispatch," Barrymore insisted. "I took it down myself, word for word. Put on your bifocals."

Collier refused to relent. "Someone is trying to double-cross us," he said menacingly, and it was clear from his expression who he thought it was. "Go back and look again. I'm sure you will find the genuine message."

"But I know this is the one, sir," Barrymore countered and, since it was a farce, he decided to go overboard. "It was sent by a well-known female impersonator."

"Then have her, or him, send us another."

"But he or she can't. He or it just died." Barrymore pretended to wipe away a tear and sniff. "Are you going to the funeral?"

"No, how can I?"

"Why not, sir?" Barrymore dared to ask.

At this point, Collier knew they were in so deep that he could no longer go back.

"Because," explained Collier logically, "I haven't got a black dress! Now go for the other message!"

Barrymore left the stage, leaving Collier to ad-lib for almost half a minute, which can feel more like a half hour to an actor. Finally Barrymore reappeared, with exactly the same tiny triangle of paper.

"Sir," Barrymore announced officiously, "I have had this authenticated." He held aloft the little scrap. "It was not written by the late female impersonator but by the very clever fellow who engraves the Lord's Prayer on the heads of pins."

Nicol Williamson is known for both his acting ability and his mercurial temperament. It was in no less a production than *Macbeth* at Stratford-upon-Avon that Williamson had one of his greatest emotional meltdowns.

It was a school matinee, and many of the children in the audience were talking to each other. Finally, Williamson's patience ran out. He slammed down the stool he was holding, told the young audience to shut up, and went on a tirade.

He informed the children that he could have been making thousands of pounds a week in a film in America instead of being in a great play by a great playwright in a great theater for next to nothing, so they could damn well be quiet while he did so.

He reminded the youthful attendees that there were some adults in the audience who had, unlike them, paid for tickets and wanted to hear what he was saying. Finally, Williamson concluded his lesson by threatening that if he heard one more whisper, he would start the play over again from the beginning and continue to do so until the entire play could be performed to the end with no sound from the audience.

This apparently frightened the students more than anything else he could have said, and the play continued to its conclusion.

But this was not Williamson's only fit of pique, by any means. Playwright-director-producer Simon Levy of the Fountain Theatre in Hollywood was at Zellerbach Auditorium in Berkeley to theoretically enjoy watching *Hamlet*.

Apparently, the temperamental Williamson took the idea of the Melancholy Dane a bit too seriously, for at one point he looked out at the audience balefully and announced, "I'm so sorry. I don't know what to say. I'm just not *feeling* it tonight. I suppose you should get your money back." And with that, he left the stage and ended the performance.

Levy and the Berkeley audience were not the only ones to suffer from Williamson's moodiness. Williamson should perhaps never have done Hamlet anywhere at any time, for the actor was in that play in Boston in 1969 when he announced, right in the middle of a scene, that he was going to end his acting career. Williamson walked offstage, but changed his mind and returned to finish the show.

That would be enough baggage for any stage star, but the worst was yet to come. Ironically, it was in Paul Rudnick's perfectly titled *I Hate Hamlet* that Williamson was at his unpardonable best.

In Rudnick's comedic work, a TV actor, played at the Walter Kerr on Broadway by Evan Handler, is apprehensive about playing Hamlet, and a séance brings back the ghost of John Barrymore (Williamson), who counsels him on how to perform the role.

Williamson, however, did a bit of counseling beyond the play, for during a dueling scene one night, he yelled at Handler, not Handler's character, and eventually drew blood, cutting Handler on the backside. Handler made an unscheduled early exit, leaving Williamson to finish the play by himself.

On closing night, after *I Hate Hamlet* was shut out of nominations for the 1991 Tony Awards, Williamson gave a seething curtain speech, lambasting the nomination process, bitterly telling a stunned crowd, "Everything about it is appalling."

Usually, the problem with a death scene during live theater is that a gunshot will not be heard or a performer will take too long to die, writhing about for additional dramatic effect.

The legendary opera tenor Enrico Caruso had a different kind of problem with a murder scene. He stabbed his costar and she refused to even fall to the floor.

It was at the Metropolitan Opera, during a production of Georges Bizet's *Carmen*, a lavish production that used live horses in the final act to pull a coach containing Carmen and Escamillo.

However, one night, one of the horses chose the moment before the stabbing death of *Carmen* to show that it was less than impressed, emptying its bowels all over the stage.

Shortly thereafter, Caruso climactically thrust a dagger into operatic star Maria Jeritza, but she refused to fall to the floor.

Caruso figured she needed one more stabbing to remind her the opera called for her to die. But Jeritza remained standing.

Over the music, Caruso, furious at this amendment of the plot, shouted at Jeritza, "Die! Fall, will you?"

"I'll die," Jeritza yelled back, "if you can find me a clean place!"

Ian Flanders, son of actor Ed Flanders, is the general manager of the Theatricum Botanicum, an outdoor theater in lush Topanga Canyon on the western edge of Los Angeles. In the 1970s, Aristophanes' *Lysistrata* was produced there and, as with other Theatricum Botanicum shows, it featured the use of live animals.

Anthony Herrera, playing the President of the Senate, entered with a flourish on the back of a donkey, which, according to Flanders, was one of the show's most reliable performers.

But that all changed one afternoon when Herrera opened his

mouth to say his first lines and was interrupted by the donkey, which suddenly sneezed. But this was no ordinary donkey sneeze. A greenish, viscous goo, with the consistency of maple syrup, covered the donkey's snout.

Herrera, along with actor Peter Alsop, continued the scene, but the disgusting image of the mucus-covered donkey made audience members in the front of the amphitheatre giggle.

Finally, disturbed by the less-than-pleasing image and the sporadic laughter from the patrons, Alsop decided to add a line to *Lysistrata*: "I think," he said, looking at the donkey, "your ass needs wiping."

The audience lost it. When the deed was done by a stagehand and the laughter subsided, Herrera respectfully replied, "Thanks for wiping my ass," and was greeted with more hysterics from the crowd.

Jenifour Jones and Kathryn Foreman run GoGetIt.org, a special-event company specializing in romantic adventures. For one of their most remarkable schemes, they created a hoax, an off-Broadway show that purposely played for only one night in order to help a client deliver a customized marriage proposal.

Alex Hamerman told the company that Gigi, his intended, was obsessed with TV host and relationship guru Dr. Phil, as well as the fairy tale *The Frog Prince*. So, Jones and Foreman not only created a play that addressed Gigi's preferences, they booked the Producer's Club in Manhattan, printed up phony playbills, and planted 100 audience members, who supposedly paid $45 to see the smash hit *Finding Prince Charming*.

An actor in a frog outfit was featured in the play, as was the character of Dr. Phil. When Gigi's name was drawn from a hat during an audience participation section, she was whisked onstage in front of the "audience" and dressed up like a princess.

The house was lit by candles. After a few minutes, the frog character, which had disappeared for a while, reappeared onstage. Off came the head of the frog costume, magically revealing the face of Alex Hamerman, who, still dressed like a frog, though behaving like a prince, presented Gigi with a diamond ring and asked her to marry him.

Shocked and delighted, she shouted "yes" a few times, just to make sure there was no misunderstanding.

Finding Prince Charming closed then and there, easily the most successful one-night run in off-Broadway history.

As everyone is entitled to an opinion, so is everyone entitled to write a play. But there are certain plays that should rightfully never be staged.

British bookseller Samuel Ireland was a devoted fan of the works of Shakespeare. So his delight knew no bounds when, in 1794, his son, William Henry, brought home from the law office where he worked a mortgage signed by the Bard himself. The eighteen-year-old told his father he'd found the document in the estate papers of a client who wished to remain anonymous.

William Henry Ireland went on to please his father even more, for his continued exploration into Shakespeareana yielded other remarkable finds, including a love letter to Anne Hathaway and, most significantly, a historical drama, previously unproduced, entitled *Vortigern*.

It was arranged to have *Vortigern* premiere at the Drury Lane on April 2, 1796. The theater's owner was not convinced the play had really been written by Shakespeare, but the public interest, and ticket sales, convinced him to overlook his doubts.

The actors, however, were not as easily swayed. They clearly felt the writing was not on a par with Shakespeare's known plays. On opening night, they broadly exaggerated their roles, and when lead actor John Philip Kemble arrived at the line "And when this solemn mockery is ended . . ." he delivered it with so much overemphasis that the audience knew he was referring to the play. It brought a loud chorus of laughter and derisive applause.

The play was never performed again. A few weeks later, William Henry Ireland confessed that *Vortigern*—and all the other documents—were his own. Alas, all's well that ends well, and the young man's career as a playwright began and ended in one night.

Samuel Ireland, however, whether due to family pride or madness, refused to believe his son's confession and to his dying day insisted that the documents and play were the work of the Bard of Avon.

When something unexpected happens in live theater, a clever ad-lib by an actor can usually ameliorate the situation, and even elicit laughter and applause. It is rare that an improvised line by an actor makes the audience cringe, but it does happen.

Bob Gutowski was in attendance at the Winter Garden Theater for a Broadway preview of *Doctor Jazz*. This musical by Buster Davis and Luther Henderson had a revisionist theme. It was about the man who invented jazz, who turned out to be white (Bobby Van), and his lover and protégée, played by Lola Falana.

During a Las Vegas–style number, with Falana leading other dancers in skimpy outfits, the exertion of the dance broke one of the straps on her costume and out tumbled one of her breasts. Despite this embarrassment, she kept dancing, keeping the exposed body part covered with one hand while gamely going through her moves.

A transition to another scene meant that Falana had no time to fix her outfit. She was in an emotionally moving scene with Van, discussing their relationship.

Shattering the mood, Van started off by leering at Falana, who was still holding her costume up with one hand.

He giggled and, leaving the text of the book, asked, "Do you really want to be a star?"

Surprised by the question and wanting to get through the crisis, Falana helpfully replied, "Um, yes!"

"OK," said Van. "Just put down your hand!"

The line was met by general silence, not the hilarious laughter Van hoped for.

After forty-two previews, *Doctor Jazz* opened and closed after five performances. Despite that, the talented Falana got a Tony nomination for Best Actress in a Musical. The rather crude Bobby Van got this anecdote.

Fisher Stevens played Jigger Craigin in a revival of *Carousel* at the Vivian Beaumont in Lincoln Center, and in a scene that takes place during a clambake, the townspeople are supposed to be upset. But they had to hide their laughter after Stevens had trouble with Oscar Hammerstein's lyrics.

Stevens was supposed to sing, "Stonecutters cut it on stone / Woodpeckers peck it on wood."

One show, he sang, "Stonecutters cut it on wood." The ensemble froze in anticipation of the next line. Stevens gave *Carousel* a unique sexual twist as he sang, "Woodpeppers perk it on porn."

During a problem with lines, some actors have the innate ability to make up text. This is impressive where contemporary speech is concerned, but even more so when the play being performed is from a different era.

During World War II, when there was a definite lack of players available for the stage in England, Peter Ustinov directed and starred as Sir Anthony Absolute in Sheridan's *The Rivals*. Dame Edith Evans played the delightful Mrs. Malaprop, but Ustinov had to use both civilian and military personnel as actors. The show toured garrisons, where it was not possible to hide the orchestra from view.

And the orchestra Ustinov was saddled with was unique, including eight players from the Berlin Philharmonic and seven from the Vienna Philharmonic. They often passed the time, before their next musical cue, playing chess with each other.

One night, Evans noticed a man on all fours, in the orchestra, playing chess. This so startled her that she completely forgot where she was in the play. Befuddled, she looked at Ustinov and asked, "What did you say?"

Ustinov dug down into the miraculous recesses of his creativity and, without thinking, the following words, which Sheridan had never written, tumbled out of his mouth:

"Madam, though the humors of bath be but a diversion to our contumely, I will not presume upon your generosity to the extent of belittling those very qualities which, while they do us but scant justice before the evil tongues of the town, nevertheless becalm the odious and bring success to fools."

And with that, Ustinov left the stage. The audience burst into applause, even though they didn't really understand what he had just said.

There is a good reason for plays to have out-of-town tryouts. If a disaster happens, there's still time to straighten it out before Broadway.

Director Philip Moeller was part of one of those virtual disasters. It was the Boston tryout for S. N. Behrman's 1929 play *Meteor*, about a ruthless businessman corrupted by power. Perhaps Moeller himself was subject to the same vices, for he vehemently criticized Behrman and harangued actors Alfred Lunt and Lynn Fontanne, and, during previews, he and Behrman both stormed out of the theater, furious with each other. With only a matter of hours before the play was to go onstage, neither one had settled how Behrman would rewrite the third act of the show.

Lunt went to Theatre Guild manager Theresa Helburn and told her, "We can't play tonight. This play doesn't have an ending."

The show was sold out, and Helburn insisted it would go on,

come hell or high water. Lunt and Helburn decided he would extemporize at the very end of *Meteor* and, when he said a certain word, the stage manager would immediately bring the curtain down.

Their plan worked perfectly, preventing *Meteor* from crashing on the heads of an unsuspecting Boston public.

The word was *schlemiel.*

Neil Simon's comedies are legendary. Perhaps his most serious play, *The Gingerbread Lady*, deals with alcoholism. And one night, onstage with Shelley Winters, Diane Hurley found herself ready to hit the bottle.

Winters played the alcoholic Evy Meara and Hurley was Toby Landau, a friend trying to exert a positive influence on her. One night, when the two women were in the middle of a scene at Chicago's Water Tower Theatre, Winters suddenly announced, "I've got to go now," and left the stage. There were still pages to go in the scene.

Stunned, Hurley wondered what to do next. The stage manager tried to bail her out by ringing the onstage telephone. Hurley walked over to it, desperately trying to think of which character she would not face in the third act. In what Hurley described as "the longest forty-five seconds of my life," she created a one-sided phone conversation, complaining about the character Evy.

Then, Winters's voice was heard offstage, announcing her re-entry. Winters entered. Hurley look at her with fury.

"Are you angry with me?" Winters asked, more speaking as herself than as Evy.

You're damned right, thought Hurley. She improvised a speech about Evy's alcoholism, her irresponsibility, including her leaving without saying where she was going. Then the two actresses got back to Simon's text and completed the play.

Backstage, Hurley demanded to know why Winters had left the scene early.

"Oh, honey," purred Winters apologetically. "I had to take my girdle off. I just couldn't stand it."

Theater historian Miles Krueger was present for a bit of theater history during the show *Portofino* at New York's Adelphi Theater in 1958. Krueger was at the Saturday matinee, after the Friday opening night, with a then twenty-year-old singer named Bobby Short. They witnessed not only a musical that was not ready to be performed, but a female lead who was not afraid to admit it . . . onstage.

Helen Gallagher had apparently read the writing on the wall during the opening night performance. By the time the cast had lumbered through the first act that Saturday afternoon, it was clear the audience was less than enthralled. Gallagher was none too excited herself. During a scene when actor Georges Guétary, as a dead race-car driver, was carried off by a dancer playing the Devil, Gallagher could not stop herself from involuntarily laughing.

Sensing *Portofino*'s destiny, Gallagher amazed the audience by breaking character and asking, plaintively, "How much more of this crap do you want? Do you want to go to the finale?"

The audience, sensing a rare opportunity not to be missed, applauded, and the orchestra went to the finale, which was performed, thereby cutting the show short.

And on the topic of cutting the show short, *Portofino* closed that night, after its third performance.

Elaine May and Mike Nichols are heralded as one of the greatest improv and comedy teams ever. But one night, even these two gifted performers unconsciously went to a very disturbing place onstage.

When they performed at the Compass Players in Chicago, the predecessor to Second City, Nichols and May used to do a bit called "Pirandello." Inspired by that playwright's *Six Characters in Search of an Author*, the sketch worked like this: First, Nichols and May would be children, imitating their parents. Then, they would become the parents, fighting in earnest. Then they would become Nichols and May, fighting with each other about performing Pirandello. Then, as the audience grew uncomfortable, May would start to leave the stage, angry. Nichols would grab at her blouse.

"What do you think you're doing?" May would demand, infuriated.

"Pirandello," Nichols would blithely reply and they would both take a bow, showing the astonished audience it was all part of the sketch.

The daring of this concept viscerally affected its audiences, but none more so than the night Nichols and May got to the point in "Pirandello" when they were pretending to fight with each other. Both got lost in the intensity of the moment and actually began to hurt each other. Nichols hit May, while May clawed at his chest.

Offstage, both broke down in tears.

In 1943, actor-writer-director Harold Kennedy put together a program of three short plays under the program title *Three Curtains*. He had everything lined up for an eventual New York opening. He had Gloria Swanson starring; the show had great reviews on the road; and it had the support of Elliot Norton, the dean of Boston theater critics, when it opened there.

Alas, the evening also had a bizarre Czech actor named Francis Lederer.

First, in rehearsals, Lederer, playing a Scottish soldier in J. M. Barrie's *The Old Lady Shows Her Medals*, kept spitting on the floor, much to the disgust of Swanson. Kennedy explained to Lederer that he had to stop spitting. Lederer argued that a soldier would very naturally spit, but Kennedy did not relent.

"You are worse than Katherine Cornell," said Lederer, who had previously toured with that actress. "At least she had some excuse, because it used to get on the hem of her gowns."

Opening night was well received in Boston and it appeared the show was destined for Broadway. Kennedy and Swanson had been highly praised by Norton, but Lederer did not get such good treatment in the review. This might have been why on the second night Lederer had a meltdown on stage that is unparalleled, even given the histrionic nature of actors.

During the first of the three plays, Shaw's *The Man of Destiny*, Kennedy made his usual entrance, pounding on an offstage door to a tavern and waiting for Lederer, as a young Napoleon Bonaparte, to open it. On that night, when Lederer opened the door, the first lines out of his mouth were his own, not Shaw's: "Oh, you have read the notices. You are now the star of the play."

Neither Kennedy nor the audience could at first comprehend the treachery and lack of professionalism Lederer was exhibiting. But it wasn't over.

Swanson entered the scene from a staircase on the opposite side of the stage and delivered her first line to Lederer.

Apparently, Lederer resented Swanson's good notices, too. "Myah, myah, myah," he uttered viciously, making fun of the rhythm of her speech.

Swanson, staring down at him imperiously and hatefully, delivered another line Shaw had not thought up. "If you open your mouth again, I will give you such a slap in the face."

Norton had come to the show a second time, as he was writing a piece in the Sunday edition of the *Boston Post*. He arrived backstage just in time to see Swanson, in tears, shout, "I will never walk on the stage with that man again!"

A banner headline on the front page of the *Post* on Sunday read, "Backstage Row Threatens to Close Play."

That evening, while Kennedy and Swanson had a late-night supper in her hotel suite, Lederer, who clearly was in the habit of reading the local papers, burst in, had a terrible shouting match with his co-star and director, and had to be escorted out by a hotel detective.

Kennedy and Swanson agreed to close the play the next week, preventing it from ever getting to New York.

One of the many challenges of the acting trade is memorizing rewrites of plays, sometimes at the very last minute. First productions are especially tricky, and that is what actor Cotter Smith had to deal with when Mark Medoff's *The Majestic Kid* premiered at Colorado's Snowmass Festival.

On the morning of the opening, Medoff gave Smith a new

version of the monologue that closed the play and asked if the actor could memorize it in time for the performance that night. Smith said he would try, but would also bring a printed copy with him in case he forgot any lines. Medoff agreed, preferring that the new speech be read rather than the old one, which he did not like, be recited.

On opening night, Smith moved downstage and addressed the audience, delivering the new speech. He got a third of the way through before it became inextricably entwined with the old speech. He stopped performing and explained to the audience what had happened and that he would now read the speech from a piece of paper he had brought with him.

But Smith searched all his pockets and could not find the speech. He stood there, unsure what to do. Finally, he called out into the void.

"Mark, are you out there?"

"Yes, I'm here," called back Medoff from the back of the theater.

"Can you talk me through this speech?" Smith asked. And the audience was treated to the playwright feeding the monologue to the actor, as they worked together, one delivering part of a line, the other completing it, to the end of the play.

Sandy Wilson wrote lyrics for Hermione Gingold's solo show *Slings and Arrows* in 1948 and they reappeared in a revue called *See You Later* at the Watergate in London. While Gingold in her performance displayed rhyme, reason was not forthcoming.

The sketch in question concerned a seventeenth-century night watchman, who intoned, as an opening line, "Twelve o'clock and everything's ghastly."

The line turned out to be prophetic. Later, Wilson wrote the line, "Hush, hush, whisper who dares / Christopher Wren is saying his prayers."

Gingold's version came out, "Hush, hush, whisper who dares / Christopher Wren is designing some stairs."

Gingold had designs on more of Wilson's lyrics in the sketch "Medusa." He had written, "He wooed me in every conceivable shape / As a horse, as a bull, as a bear, as an ape."

Apparently, Gingold was particularly hungry when she sang out, "He wooed me in every conceivable shape / As a horse, as a bull, as a bear, as a grape."

Sometimes it is not a matter of an actor forgetting lines but of he or she being unable to pronounce certain words, despite hours of rehearsal.

No less an actor than Ralph Richardson was in Joe Orton's outrageous comedy *What the Butler Saw* during its pre-London tour. In fact, Richardson, according to Coral Browne, never learned what certain words in the play meant. For example, the word "nymphomaniac" always seemed to come out onstage as "nymphzomaniac."

Richardson clearly knew he was at sea, and when Peter O'Toole and Peggy Ashcroft came to his dressing room on separate occasions to congratulate him, he used the same line on each of them:

"Do either of you have a little cyanide?"

David Ferry was about to be tortured with a hot branding iron onstage one night in J. M. Synge's *Playboy of the Western World.* It was Theatre Calgary in 1976 and Ferry was playing Christy Mahon. At the end of the play, a rope has been put around his neck and the townspeople are jeering at him because he has falsely claimed to have killed his own father.

To make their hatred of Christy complete, Pegeen Flaherty, the strong-willed woman who wanted to love him, prepares to scorch him with the iron.

"You're blowin' for to torture me," says Mahon in the play.

"You're fixin' for to blow me," said Ferry onstage.

Suddenly the townspeople were laughing, walking off and then back onstage to hide their laughter. Never did a condemned man so quickly change the mood of a murderous crowd.

Lady Diana Rigg had to keep a stiff upper lip when acting in that most dramatic of plays, *King Lear*. She was Cordelia and Paul Scofield was Lear in Peter Brook's production at Stratford-upon-Avon.

While *Lear* is not generally known as a comedy, the whole show nearly came undone when Scofield diverted amusingly from the text. In act 4, scene 6, when the two characters are reunited and sympathetically discuss how much they resent Lear's other two daughters, Rigg declaimed, "Had you not been their father, these white flakes did challenge pity of them."

Under his breath, Scofield impishly said, "Are you suggesting I've got dandruff?"

James Duffy and Fred Sweeney, a comedy duo of yesteryear, were in

30

the habit of hitting each other and insulting their audience in order to get laughs, which they did most of the time.

But not in Memphis, Tennessee, where the audience was as silent as a tomb. All their best lines failed. So Duffy, no longer able to stand the silence, decided to get some kind of reaction.

He walked down to the footlights, peered out into the darkness, and delivered the following heartfelt speech:

"Citizens of Memphis! This is one of the happiest and proudest moments of our lives. Your reception has been overwhelming. And now, please remain in your seats a few minutes longer, while my partner, Mr. Sweeney, passes down the aisle with a baseball bat and beats the be-Jesus out of you."

The management quickly stopped the show.

The grand and grandiose actor Sir Donald Wolfit had a way with words, even if they were not part of the play.

His great passion was performing Shakespeare, but his respect for the Bard was suspect during the production of *Twelfth Night* in which he cut an entire scene, of Malvolio in prison. To the person brave enough to ask him why, offstage, he explained, "I cannot learn it, and if I cannot learn it, Shakespeare did not write it."

Another time, in Belfast, Wolfit lay dying onstage as *Othello*. The young actor who was to confirm the Moor's death before the next line leaned down close to Wolfit, who was stock-still.

It came as a shock, then, when the previously dead Othello

opened his mouth and whispered, "My boy, you must do something about your breath."

Heather Summerhayes will never forget the tour she and her husband, Richard McMillan, did for Young People's Theatre throughout Canada. They were performing for public school children in various gymnasiums, doing a play called *Almighty Voice and His Wife*.

McMillan played a Canadian Mountie who was chasing the elusive Indian Almighty Voice. At the most dramatic moment, with hundreds of kids hanging on his every word, McMillan was to order a subordinate to prepare his horse as he risked his life to capture the Indian.

The line, as written, was: "Get my mount ready, Constable Dickson."

It came out: "Get my cunt ready, Mountable Dickson!"

The schoolchildren laughed for ten minutes, and a few teachers fainted.

Tony Rosato took LSD for the first time, according to him, in the late 1970s or early 1980s. One assumes it did not affect his memory.

One point Rosato is quite clear on is that when he was first given acid, it was hours before a performance with the Second City Toronto improv troupe. His girlfriend and her sisters assured him it would leach out of his system in a couple of hours and have no affect on his show.

Rosato had every reason to believe them, because he felt no

effects whatever during the day. It was fate that Rosato was in the middle of an improv bit onstage when the psychedelic drug finally took hold of his mind and yanked him all over the map. Rosato felt he should have known it would eventually take hold, as his girlfriend and her sisters were laughing at moments in the show no one else found funny.

Rosato was playing a cab driver and fellow Second City member Ditch Dickerson was an out-of-towner who was arriving at Union Station and was on his way to his hotel, the Royal York, which is, in reality, directly across the street from Union Station.

As Rosato pantomimed driving, he was amazed that instead of just pretending to drive, he was actually experiencing the sensations of driving—of braking, accelerating, signaling, and seeing other cars and buildings and pedestrians.

This reverie was interrupted by an abrupt punch on the shoulder. Behind him, Dickerson angrily whispered, "Tony, where the fuck are you? Stop driving. The scene is going on."

Rosato had been driving in real time, spending minutes off in his own world, while Dickerson was trying to get him to say something.

The drug now convinced Rosato that honesty was the best policy. "You'll have to excuse me, man. I just dropped some acid before I came in today."

The audience laughed, not recognizing the confession for what it was.

Then a waitress loudly dropped a tray of drinks. Rosato's attention was suddenly diverted and, in the grand style of improvisation, using everything and anything around them, Rosato demanded to know what a cocktail waitress was doing in the middle of a highway. They created jokes based on that for a while, and then Dickerson accidentally dropped his lit cigarette-not a prop but a real, burning cigarette-onto Rosato's shirt. Rosato, still seeing the beauty and wonder in everything around him, made some jokes with Dickerson about the cigarette while it was still smoldering. Rosato found himself fascinated by the colors of the burning cigarette end, even though his shirt was beginning to smolder, too.

Finally, yanked back reluctantly to the reality of the stage, Rosato "drove" Dickerson to the door of his hotel. Rosato the cabbie had taken a very circuitous route, but the reward was a great round of applause.

Afterward, Rosato was told by others it was the best sketch he had ever done. They did not know how he had researched the role of a cab driver on LSD.

Until 1968, all plays performed in England were submitted to Lord Chamberlain for licensing. The governmental office, a holdover from the Tudor period, was there to delete or change any language that was obscene or blasphemous, or that might otherwise offend the monarch.

When Edward Albee's *Who's Afraid of Virginia Woolf?* traveled to London, the words "Jesus Christ," which are sprinkled throughout, were limited to three utterances.

Uta Hagen's opening line as Martha, "Jesus H. Christ," was censored by Lord Chamberlain. So Albee changed it to "Mary H. Magdalene," which was accepted. But Hagen, used to performing it a certain way for a year, messed up the line on opening night, declaring, "Jesus H. Magdalene!"

The phrase "hump the hostess" was allowed, because *hump* had been used by Shakespeare with the same sexual connotation. But the clinical word "scrotum" was disallowed. Arthur Hill was forced to say that he was having an operation "on the underside of my privacies." But after struggling with this on their first night in London, Hill refused to say it again.

On the subject of the family jewels, the office of the Lord Chamberlain particularly found offense in the phrase "She was his left ball." Albee rejected the substitutions "nut" and "testicle." Then he recalled the old Southern expression of having "a right bawl," or cry. Albee changed the spelling. Lord Chamberlain could not object, and the sanctity of the written word in theater was maintained.

Comedian George Jessel was noted as a toastmaster at the famed Friars Club and other venues. Once, at a tribute dinner for Maurice Chevalier, the movie studio head Jesse Lasky kept losing his place in his speech. It was obvious it had been written for him and Lasky was ruining the spontaneity of the event. Each time he lost his place, Lasky would mutter, "Now where was I?"

Finally, after one pause too many, Jessel helped Lasky find his place.

"You're at the Hotel Astor," Jessel groused, "and your name is Jesse Lasky."

Jessel formulated the best rule for after-dinner speeches: "It should be like a woman's skirt," he explained, "just long enough and short enough to cover the subject."

But at a birthday banquet for New York's controversial mayor Jimmy Walker, Judge Mitchell May went on and on, without end, delivering a speech that threatened to turn the audience into fossils.

When the judge reached for a glass of water during a momentary pause in his blathering, Jessel quickly stepped in, bringing things to a sudden but welcome close.

"As this is Mayor Walker's birthday," Jessel cagily summed up, "let's all hope he lives as long as Mitchell May's speech."

Jean Arthur was trying to make a comeback. She had been cast in the lead in Garson Kanin's *Born Yesterday* but got sick at the last minute during the Boston tryout and backed out of the role.

Cheryl Crawford, one of the three founders of the Group Theatre, should have seen the writing on the wall. The musical she was producing in 1967 for Arthur's return to the stage was entitled *The Freaking Out of Stephanie Blake.*

Crawford was not totally naive. She wanted verbal assurances from Arthur that if she performed in the musical by Richard Chandler and Jeff Barry, there would not be a repeat visitation of a sudden, vague illness. Arthur gave her those assurances. Crawford should have had a lien placed on Arthur's home and bank account.

Sure enough, the third day of previews became *The Freaking Out of Jean Arthur.* The star of so many delightful screwball comedy films simply could not handle the pressure of live performance. In the middle of the show, she got down on her knees and told the audience she could not go on and, furthermore, that her doctor had advised her to not perform.

But when Arthur got offstage, planning her latest escape, she was met by Crawford, who insisted she honor her word and, parenthetically, the contract she had signed. With no great enthusiasm,

Arthur returned to the stage moments later, but before performing, she addressed the crowd:

"I am told that I must go on and I'm going to, because I believe in the show . . . but if something happens . . ."

Nothing happened, except that no one liked the show, it closed after that performance, and Crawford condemned Arthur for losing her 1967 investment of $250,000.

Jimmy Durante performed in a Rodgers and Hart musical called *Jumbo* at New York's Hippodrome Theatre in 1935. The Hippodrome at that time was billed as the largest theater in the world, seating about 5,300 people. It starred Durante and an even bigger star, Tuffy the elephant, playing Jumbo, the enormous pachyderm made popular by circus impresario P. T. Barnum.

One day, in front of an audience of thousands, Durante dropped his lines as he was taken aback by Tuffy dropping something else, in great quantity, on the stage.

Regaining his composure, Durante admonished the elephant, "Hey, Tuffy, no ad-libbing!"

The best mistakes in the theater are the ones that prompt lines and actions to cover them that become as successful as anything in the show.

Eddie Cantor was in a musical called *Banjo Eyes* at the Hollywood Theatre in New York. It was written by Joe Quillan and Izzy Ellinson who, just before it opened, added a new scene. In it, nerdy

Erwin Trowbridge (Cantor) is mistakenly drafted into the armed services. He is handed a uniform many sizes too large and ordered to put it on.

Cantor was handed a major gift on Christmas Day 1941, when *Banjo Eyes* opened. The enormous pants were put on and Cantor turned his back to the audience to zip them up.

The zipper stuck.

Desperate, Cantor yelled over his shoulder, "Someone get me a plumber!"

It was so well received, the line stayed in for the rest of the run.

Mae West returned to the Broadway stage after a long absence in 1944 with a play she wrote, *Catherine Was Great*. The queen of sexual double entendre was responsible one night for an ad-lib that is used, in different forms, to this day.

The actor playing Lieutenant Bunin, one of her many lovers in the script, got caught in his sword and scabbard at one point.

His unplanned entanglement prompted West to drawl suggestively, "Is that your sword or are you just happy to see me?"

Her curtain speech, opening night, was also memorable. "Catherine had three hundred lovers. I did the best I could in a couple of hours."

Florenz Ziegfeld is known as the theater's flashiest showman. His *Follies* featured some of the great names of the stage, including W. C. Fields, Sophie Tucker, Will Rogers, and many beautiful women who went on to have major film careers, including Irene Dunne, Paulette Goddard, and Marion Davies.

One of Ziegfeld's most spectacular moments onstage was not even part of the show, although the audience did not know it. The impresario was known to have engaged in many extramarital affairs while he was married to performer Billie Burke. One of those dalliances was with *Follies* regular Lillian Lorraine, who was performing in the first officially titled *Ziegfeld's Follies* at the Jardin de Paris on the Champs-Elysées in 1911.

During that run, the audience was treated to the usual larger-than-life menu of singing, dancing, comedy, and eye-popping stagecraft. But one night, the increasingly overbearing Lorraine got into a backstage disagreement with Fanny Brice while the production was going great guns in front.

It turned into a physical fight, and Brice got the better of Ziegfeld's mistress, knocking her down and then, as the coup de grâce, dragging her by her hair across the stage of the Jardin de Paris. This was met with the roaring approval of the audience, who assumed it was just another blockbuster moment orchestrated by the ingenious Ziegfeld.

Lorraine missed a rehearsal soon after, and coproducer A. L. Erlanger convinced Ziegfeld to fire her. Lorraine would be rehired—and refired—before her association with Ziegfeld came to an end.

It is interesting to note the comedians that comedy writers and performers like best. The great humorist James Thurber went on record as saying the funniest line he ever heard was from Fred Allen, performing in a vaudeville house.

Allen stopped his prepared material after spotting a very thin and pale cellist in the orchestra pit.

Allen moved toward him, studied the man carefully, and then asked, "How much would you charge to haunt a house?"

Actors must often memorize reams of material, and it's hard not to feel sympathetic when an actor "goes up" or "dries." But how much understanding should one muster when an entire cast forgets where it is in a play?

Susan Hogan was onstage in Tom Walmsley's *White Boys* at the Tarragon Theatre in Toronto. Joining her were David McIlwraith, Michael Hogan, and Patrick Brymer. The dialogue was zipping along at a pleasant pace.

Then, all of a sudden, as if a death ray had been focused upon the stage, all the talking ceased. The four actors looked at one another, waiting for a cue from someone to break the impasse.

It was that rare theatrical moment, so unique no one has named it until right now: "Simultaneous quadruple brain lock." None of the actors knew where they were or how to proceed.

McIlwraith solved the problem in that warm and giving, time-honored fashion: he left the stage. Susan collated papers in front of her and hummed some tune, as the play hung in suspended animation. Then she too left the battlefield.

Brymer sat in his chair, staring straight ahead, as if lobotomized. Michael did some inane stage business, playing with a swinging door, as they all waited for inspiration. None was forthcoming. Michael then left the stage, leaving Brymer, alone, staring out into some private hell.

Susan got on a headset and spoke with the stage manager, Larry Farley, and told him they had all left themselves high and dry.

The four actors assembled again onstage, waiting, as if in some new but not very well-paced Pirandello play.

Finally, the voice of Farley boomed out over the speakers in the theater, informing the cast and everyone else exactly where they were in the play.

"You're at the bottom of page forty-three," he said, not so helpfully.

The audience cracked up, and one of the actors asked, sheepishly, "So what do we say, and who says it?"

Things really got off to a bang at one performance of Noël Coward's *Blithe Spirit* at the Neil Simon Theater. Judith Ivey was sitting properly at a table as Ruth, awaiting the entry of the maid, Edith, with sandwiches and tea.

The sandwiches and tea were promptly dropped with an enormous crash, seconds after the play had started.

Ivey, showing a stiff upper lip, intoned, "Please bring more tea, sandwiches, and unbroken china."

Then she got down on her knees and swept up the spilled sugar onstage. The maid returned, catching her in this less-than-aristocratic position. Affecting a certain pride and coming up with her second brilliant cover in about a minute, Ivey warned, "Make sure you mention this to no one, Edith."

Before Julian Fellowes was directing movies, writing books, and winning the Oscar for his screenplay *Gosford Park*, he worked as an actor in theaters throughout England. It is no wonder he has changed his emphasis, considering the treatment he got in the play *Lloyd George Knew My Father* at the Royal Theatre in Northampton. Fellowes was playing a vicar in the William Douglas Home play, and one would have expected a bit more respect than what he received during one performance. That night the leading lady, who was noted for being a bit of a lush, showed up completely plastered.

In one scene with Fellowes, she normally delivered a monologue, basically saying that her life consisted of ordering groceries and going to church. She would then turn plaintively to Fellowes and wonder if God was as bored as the grocer must be, hearing the same old list every week.

The actress, slurring her words, barely managed her lines, and concluded by blaring, "Jesus, Vicar, I wonder if God is as sick of you as I am!"

2

Who Are You Wearing?
(Costumes and Makeup)

LESLIE CROWTHER WAS a principal comedian in the *Black and White Minstrel Show* that ran from 1962 to 1965 at London's Victoria Palace. A live orchestra and taped singing were used so that the performers had ease of movement and did not have to use microphones.

But one night there was a power failure in the theater while they were in their dressing rooms before the show.

Crowther and fellow performer George Chisholm heard the taped singing of Tony Mercer change a key and then slow down, dropping lower and lower, even though the orchestra played at its usual tempo. Then all the lights went out.

Crowther and Chisholm ran in total darkness from their dressing rooms, grabbing flashlights on the run. Shining them in each other's faces, they entertained the crowd for forty-five minutes. Chisholm played the trombone impromptu and Crowther belted out jokes.

The only problem was the resolution of the problem. The power returned suddenly and the theater was flooded with light.

Crowther and Chisholm were wearing nothing but jock straps.

Charles Laughton could be difficult to work with. And in the London production of *On the Spot* by Edgar Wallace in 1930, he was playing an outlandish character named Tony Perelli. In the course of the play, he is guilty of sexual assault, betrayal, murder, pimping, and sobbing in front of a statue of the Virgin Mary.

But Laughton was not to blame for a snafu that tested his ability—or lack of same—to improvise in a tricky situation.

Gladys Frazin played a moll named Maria Poluski in *On the Spot*, and that is just where she and Laughton wound up one evening. Frazin's offstage lover, director Monte Banks, had taken her back to their apartment after the matinee for drinks and whatever else came up.

On the night in question, the final performance in London, they had an argument and Banks, in a fit of pique, threw the naked Frazin's clothes out the window. With an evening performance scheduled in just minutes, and nothing else to wear, Frazin grabbed her mink coat and ran out the door to the theater.

As bad luck would have it, Laughton's first line to Frazin when they were onstage together was, "May I take your coat?"

Frazin opened her coat slightly, allowing Laughton to see exactly why she would not be offering him her coat to hang up that evening. Laughton began to sweat visibly and struggled to find dialogue to improvise.

Frazin, upset as well, mistakenly blurted out, "Oh, Charles." The audience gasped at the error. "I mean, oh, Tony," she giggled, and the audience roared.

Tom Jacobson's play *Bunbury*, at the Road Theatre in North Hollywood, was a send-up of *Romeo and Juliet* and other well-known plays. Normally, Romeo, played by Scot M. Burklin, got laughs when he buried his face in the bosom of Rosaline (Ann Noble), Romeo's previous and short-lived love.

But one night, it became a tragedy-turned-comedy-turned-tragedy. Rosaline, uncertain about her feelings for Romeo, always pulled away when he planted his face between her breasts. Her reproach was more than verbal that evening, as the crucifix she was wearing got caught in one of his nostrils.

Burklin's nose was ripped open, and he tried to shield the audience from the blood that poured out. Alas, blood was soon dripping down his chin.

Both actors continued the scene, which culminated with a kiss and Romeo's death. The last image the audience was left with that night for this comedy, was Rosaline, with a blood mustache, standing over the inert Romeo.

The play *Amadeus* by Peter Shaffer was staged at the Source Theatre in Washington, D.C., in 1985, and Elizabeth DuVall was in the role of Constanze, Mozart's love interest, later his wife. But after the actor playing Mozart left her in a most vulnerable position, love was the last thing on her mind.

DuVall was flirting and romping about onstage as required, but when the actor playing Mozart was supposed to pick her up, he did not realize that both his feet were firmly positioned on the hem of her long dress.

DuVall was lifted skyward, but the dress was violently ripped away from the bodice. The petticoats came with it. This left DuVall wearing nothing on her bottom half but little, flowered bikini panties and blue kneepads, there to protect her from all the rolling around on the stage.

Mozart, out of keeping with his sexually voracious character, panicked at seeing the object of his affections so clothed. He muttered his last line in the scene and dashed offstage, carrying her petticoats and skirt with him.

The actor playing Salieri, Mozart's rival, was left onstage with DuVall, and they subtly made mention of her new outfit before completing the scene as rehearsed.

Undoubtedly, DuVall was not the only one who was hopping mad. The luxurious apricot silk dress had been borrowed from the Folger Theatre in Washington, D.C.

Theater critic Judd Hollander was witness to what might be labeled a "wardrobe malfunction" during a press night of Mel Brooks's *The Producers* at the St. James Theatre in 2001. However, the situation was not only saved, it was improved upon by the quicksilver brilliance of Nathan Lane playing Max Bialystock.

In one scene, Lane is wearing a bathrobe and talking to his costar, Matthew Broderick, while opening an empty safe in his office. Still talking, Lane then closes the safe and moves to another area of the stage.

But on this night, Lane closed the safe, whirled, and moved off a few steps, only to be jerked back like an errant dog on a leash. Part of the robe was caught inside the door of the safe.

Lane continued to deliver his lines and feigned trying to pull on the robe with all his might. After getting a reaction from that, he opened the safe again, freed the piece of fabric that had been safely locked away, and slammed the door shut.

As the audience laughed, Lane shouted, "It's all right!" Then, with not only the audience but Broderick watching in amazement, Lane found an empty coffee cup onstage, grabbed it, opened the safe again, tossed the cup inside, and slammed the safe door once more.

Lane then turned to Broderick and brought down the house by saying, "We have to feed this hungry safe!"

Andrea Tate will never forget her first Equity show, possibly for all the wrong reasons. She was performing in the extremely intense and dramatic *A Shayna Maidel* by Barbara Lebow. Staged at the Off Broadway Theatre in Fort Lauderdale, Florida, it concerns two Jewish sisters separated by circumstances during the Holocaust.

In the beginning of the play, one of the sisters, played by JoAnne McGee, is running from the Nazis; McGee was carrying a doll wrapped up in a blanket to stand in for her baby. There is only one thing more dramatic than a terrified woman clutching her baby to her chest as she runs from murderous Nazis.

And that one thing is when the woman is accidentally bumped by another performer onstage and tosses her "baby" into the first couple of rows of the audience.

Tate prayed that McGee would find a way to "use" this accident to make the play even more powerful, instead of getting down off the stage, going into the stalls, and asking for her plastic baby back.

But the maternal instinct took over, and McGee indeed clambered down, fetched her baby, returned to the stage, and continued to flee from the Nazis.

Hindi Brooks's play *The Night the War Came Home* started a battle between the women who staged the work and the women who ran the church, St. Ambrose, where it was performed in Hollywood.

The church ladies had assigned the cast and crew a supply closet for storage of their costumes and properties. Alas, this very closet was where the church also stored donations of clothes and other items for the poor.

Brooks had a kind costumer who lent the production two military uniforms previously worn by her father. Unfortunately, one of the women at St. Ambrose, thinking they were donations, gave them away to poor people.

As a result, *The Night the War Came Home* featured a performance in which two actors wore street clothes while, somewhere in Los Angeles, two homeless men wore military uniforms.

Comedian Cathy Ladman was scheduled to perform on New Year's Eve in Ann Arbor, Michigan. But during Christmas week, she got a gift that, so to speak, kept on giving: an upper respiratory infection. A tight travel schedule and many airline flights exacerbated her condition. By showtime in Ann Arbor, her nose was running like a faucet and the skin was bright red and raw from her dabbing at it with tissues. Even worse, she was staying at a Holiday Inn, whose tissues she described as "second in softness to tree bark."

She knew she could not keep wiping her nose while telling jokes. But the running nose kept annoying her. So, for her final show of the night, leading up to midnight, she spontaneously decided to stuff two tissues up her nose to try and stop the drainage.

The audience was so amused by her predicament, she threw out her prepared material and improvised the rest of her set on the subject of her problematic nose.

Then, at midnight, instead of blowing a noisemaker, popping open a bottle of champagne, or throwing confetti, Ladman enlisted someone in the front row of the club to come up onstage and pull the soaked tissues out of her nostrils, like a disgusting magic trick.

Funny Girl was a huge hit on Broadway with Barbra Streisand. But for one performance, it should have been renamed *Funny Guy*: on that night S. Marc Jordan, playing three roles, including the slick agent Mr. Renaldi, accidentally stole the show.

Usually, when something goes amusingly wrong during live theater, the audience laughs about it and then the show continues. But

Jordan found himself caught in a *faux pas* that kept the audience laughing, which ended up holding up the play. When normalcy was supposedly returned, the text itself conspired to throw the performers off their rhythms.

Jordan was onstage with the character Nick Arnstein, played by Sydney Chaplin. When Streisand entered, Jordan turned downstage to face her, whereupon the audience began to laugh.

Jordan looked closely at Streisand to see what was wrong with her costume. There was nothing amiss. Then he glanced at Chaplin's fly to see if it was open. It was not, but the laughter built inside the theater.

Unable to deliver any lines over the mirth, Jordan looked at the set. Nothing was amiss.

The audience was now at a fever pitch of laughter. Jordan, utterly puzzled, finally glanced down to see that his own fly was not only open, it was gaping, inviting people in the back row to laugh at him. When he turned upstage to zip himself up, the laughter reached a peak and the audience did not want to calm down.

With Streisand and Chaplin waiting to go on with the musical, Jordan walked downstage to the apron, took a deep and formal bow, and finally helped the audience get over the giggles.

But only temporarily. The audience was primed, and the book of *Funny Girl* now brought back the hysteria of the crowd. Due to the influence of Jordan's previously open fly, many lines of dialogue from Chaplin as Arnstein suddenly seemed sexually suggestive. "He's opening a new office and he wants me to come in with him." "At first I thought I wanted you, but it seems he wants me for myself."

The next day, Jordan received a telegram from the show's producer, Ray Stark:

"Congratulations. I hear a new personality emerged in last night's performance. You almost pulled a boner, but keep a stiff upper lip and fly right."

Jordan wired Stark back. "I just thought it was time," he wrote, "the showbiz world saw what I had to offer. Have you any openings for me?"

Bruce Gray's first professional acting job resulted in a hilarious disaster that would have convinced a lesser man to quit the business.

In 1961, Shaw's *Androcles and the Lion* was being staged at the Mermaid Theatre in London, and Gray was delighted to be playing a variety of supernumeraries, including a soldier, a slave, and a Christian. The tallest guard in the group was a new actor named Donald Sutherland.

The show was teamed with another Shaw one-act, *The Shewing-up of Blanco Posnet*.

Ronald Frazer was playing Blanco and Caesar in *Androcles* and, one night, he invited his good friend Laurence Olivier to come see the two one-acts.

As it turned out, Frazer came down with laryngitis at the last minute and was unable to perform. Sutherland took over the role of Blanco. Gray was assigned the part of the Retiarius, a gladiator, in *Androcles*.

His only line was, "He bet me ten *sisterces* that he would vanquish me. If I had killed him, I wouldn't have gotten the money." Even though Gray thought the line did not make sense, and even though as a Canadian actor he had to fake a Cockney accent, he felt secure in making the most of his first speaking role in the professional theater.

However, if the lines were not a problem, the costuming was. The previous actor playing the Retiarius was about thirty pounds lighter than Gray. The costume consisted of nothing more than a long leather arm protector, a helmet, yards and yards of net, a trident, and the world's tiniest black jockstrap.

No matter how he shifted the jockstrap, he could not avoid the simple fact that his privates were going to be public. As the time for his call drew near, Gray hit upon a solution. He allowed his left testicle to droop outside the jockstrap, and then took an eyebrow pencil and colored it black so that it would blend in with the scanty outfit he wore.

Onstage, the understudy for Frazer's Caesar asked Gray, at the appropriate time, "And what is your reply, gladiator?"

Gray delivered his line and the court of Rome turned upstage, trying to hide their laughter from the audience. Gray knew he had a weak Cockney accent, but he didn't think it was *that* bad.

Gray turned to the Praetorian guards who were with him on his side of the stage. It was then that Sutherland, as the tallest guard, took control of the situation. He whispered to the guard next to him, "His left ball is hanging out. Pass it on."

The eyebrow pencil on Gray's family jewel had been washed off by sweat and the latter was now clearly visible. The metal-clad guard, laughing, now turned upstage as well, and their shaking bodies sounded like silverware being dumped on the ground.

Gray turned out to the audience and shook his net, placing it in front of his crotch, while the entire cast faced upstage, trying to stop laughing.

Finally, the stage manager found some garb that was vaguely Roman, threw it on, and came onstage. He took away Gray's trident as "punishment" and led him away from a hysterical cast and a perplexed audience that included Laurence Olivier.

Charles Ludlum chose the perfect name for his theater company: "Ridiculous." In keeping with the name was their production of a send-up of Wagner's Ring cycle. Instead of *Twilight of the Gods*, or *Götterdämmerung*, Ludlum named his show *Der Ring Got Farblonjet,* which roughly translated seems to mean, "God, Is This Ring Fucked Up!"

And one night, it really was. Ludlum had created Wagner's *norn* creatures in the form of three actors all stuck inside one long piece of fabric. One of the nineteen performers playing forty roles was Ericka Brown, who went by the name "Eureka." She was in the dressing room getting ready to join her two other *norns* in costume.

Ludlum, when he wasn't onstage, liked to perform backstage for his performers. He had found a hand-carved ventriloquist's dummy at an esoteric shop not far from the Truck and Warehouse Theatre on New York's East Fourth Street. He named this dummy Walter Ego.

So there was Ludlum, pretending to be Walter Ego, talking to Eureka, who suddenly realized that she was supposed to go on as a *norn*. She ran into the wings and saw the two other *norns* about to enter the scene without her.

The trailing costume was within her reach. In the great tradition of slapstick comedy, Eureka stamped her foot on the edge of the costume. The two other *norns* stopped and jerked backward, Eureka climbed in, and off they went.

The director of a show should be the final arbiter of how a text should be performed. However, actor David Figlioli found out, while doing Tom Heggen and Joshua Logan's play *Mister Roberts,* that on some occasions the director should at all costs be ignored.

While studying theater at Wayne State University, Figlioli was fortunate enough to be cast as Ensign Pulver in the play and, on opening night, despite his jitters, all the laughs came at the right places.

Figlioli was backstage waiting for his next entrance when director Blair Anderson, whom Figlioli has described as being rather fond of Scotch, saw Figlioli, panicked, and called two dressers. To Figlioli's confusion, Anderson insisted the dressers were late and needed to change Figlioli's costume immediately.

The scene he was supposed to enter was set after the laundry room on the ship had blown up. The dressers rapidly helped Figlioli into tattered clothes, supposedly shredded by the explosion. They applied black soot all over his face and soap suds everywhere.

As they finished the last touches of soot and soap suds, Figlioli suddenly froze in horror. He heard the dialogue onstage and announced calmly, but with the air of a man going to his own execution, "It's the wrong scene."

"No, it's not," insisted Anderson.

Figlioli took a beat, listened a bit longer to the actors, and repeated his assertion that it was the wrong scene, that he was not supposed to enter—and certainly not looking like he had been caught in a laundry-room explosion.

Figlioli began frantically stripping off the ripped costume. His cue to enter the scene was heard from the stage and he ad-libbed from the wings while trying to pull his uniform back on.

But one of the dressers realized his face was still covered in black soot. She spit in her hands and desperately tried to wash it off while the actors onstage kept talking.

Finally, the dressers approved Figlioli's entrance.

After the show, he told his family, who had come for the opening night, what had happened, and was relieved to hear that no one had noticed anything wrong.

Except for his mother. "Oh," she said, "I wondered why you were so dirty when you came in for that scene."

A Christmas Carol is one of the most frequently performed plays during the December holiday season. At one memorable performance at San Diego Repertory Theatre at the Lyceum, however, the Ghost of Christmas Present almost burned to death and turned into a real ghost.

Doug Roberts, as the Ghost, was wearing a costume filled with electrical lights during a 2004 matinee. There was a malfunction, and suddenly the Ghost of Christmas Present had smoke coming out of him. Peter Van Norden, playing Scrooge, started to make small gestures toward Roberts, who interpreted this as a sign that Van Norden had forgotten his own lines and needed help.

Other actors came out and began singing and dancing, not noticing that the Ghost of Christmas Present was on fire. Thankfully, the stage manager, in the booth, did, and he turned on the house lights. The backstage assistant stage manager ran to get a fire extinguisher.

Amazingly, the performers were so committed to their roles, singing and dancing, they did not stop, despite the house lights coming on and the ASM appearing on the scene with a fire extinguisher. Roberts was still clueless, thinking that some fog effect was being tried out without his previous knowledge.

Van Norden, as Scrooge, passionately made flailing arm gestures toward the burning Roberts, finally whispering, "You're on fire."

Roberts made no response, assuming that Van Norden was complimenting him on his performance thus far.

It was only when the ASM blasted Roberts with a shower of goop from the fire extinguisher that Roberts finally realized he was aflame. The singing continued, however, as Roberts fell to the floor, rolled over and over, and stripped the light-studded, incendiary costume from his body.

Theater has the power to make an audience laugh or cry. But Steven Buntrock was in a production of Rodgers and Hammerstein's *South Pacific* that unintentionally made people scream in terror.

Buntrock, as Lt. Cable, was supposed to be shot, and for that purpose, there was a blood packet under his T-shirt that he would smack and break open at the proper time.

During rehearsals, the director wasn't convinced, and he instructed Buntrock to turn toward the audience after the supposed shot so they could see the spread of "blood" through his shirt.

For the fourth show of the tour, ten minutes before the curtain, the producer had an even better idea. He told Buntrock, "We can't see enough blood through your T-shirt. Take the blood packet out and smack it on your face during the death scene."

So Buntrock hid the packet in his hand and when the shot went off, he had his back to the audience. He smashed the fist-sized packet against his head. The audience screamed in horror. It looked like Buntrock had half of his head blown off.

The effect was so startling, even for the performers, that the gun was accidentally dropped into the audience as the lights went out. Buntrock was now supposed to exit through an aisle in the house, but the mock blood, made of colored shampoo, got in his eyes and blinded him.

He stumbled into the audience in the dark, getting fake blood all over people. The gun was necessary for the performance and so the actor playing Emile De Beque went into the audience, in the dark, to try and retrieve it.

There, covered in stage blood, he reached down for what he thought was the gun.

When the lights came up, he was holding a white leather purse, now slathered in fake blood. The lady to whom it belonged was trying to grab it back.

Marissa Jaret Winokur came a long way to win her Tony for the musical *Hairspray.*

She had once been in an instructional children's theater piece called *Fiber Girl.* The purpose of the show was to teach kids how important it is to eat foods high in fiber.

Winokur's unforgettable moment on the stage came during a dance routine, while the cast sang a song about fiber and how it helped you "move."

Her costume was, as Winokur herself described it, "a dancing piece of shit with a hard hat."

It is a marvel how performers bare their souls when they do their best work. Ann Crumb had to bare more than her soul one night in

Aspects of Love, when her costume disappeared and she performed a number of different scenes in just her underwear.

In Andrew Lloyd Webber's musical, mounted at New York's Broadhurst Theatre, Crumb was playing Rose Vibert, a temperamental French actress. It was a show with twenty-three costume changes, and the one that Crumb will never forget came when she took off a period costume for a play within the play and sat onstage wearing a dainty little teddy. It was then that Michael Ball, as handsome young Englishman Alex Dillingham, entered and Crumb asked him to get a dress off the rack for her.

The only problem was, there was no dress on the rack. This oversight by the costume crew forced Crumb and Ball to rush off as is into the next scene, a café. Ball had to hide his laughter as Crumb casually sat in the public bistro wearing lingerie.

Next, per the blocking, she ran offstage and was handed a suitcase, for the characters were now to begin a traveling sequence. Crumb desperately looked inside the suitcase offstage. No dress. No time to change.

The following scene found Crumb and Ball on a train. The conductor handed her flowers, as per usual, but could not stifle his laughter.

The song on the train could not have been more apt. It was "Seeing Is Believing."

Aspects of Love now placed these two lovers on the side of a mountain, and the laughter hit new heights. Even the conductor, watching Crumb climb the mountain in her teddy, shook with laughter.

The final scene placed Ball and Crumb in France, breaking into an estate. There was a big, fifteen-minute seduction scene, which included Ball miming taking off a dress that Crumb was no longer wearing. The audience howled. Finally, Ball leaned down onto Crumb's prone body, the lights went out, and Crumb's agony was at last relieved.

Shari Albert was fortunate enough to attend New York University's Tisch School of the Arts, one of the great training centers for stage performers in the United States. Fortune also smiled on her when she was cast as Amazon Queen Hippolyta, the lead in the Rodgers and Hart musical *By Jupiter.*

What was not so lucky was her performing three numbers on opening night in leotards, without underwear. It didn't help that her mother and father were in attendance.

When the NYU student newspaper came out with its review of the show, the headline read, "Amazon Queen Rules without Pants."

On the subject of not wearing underwear, Tallulah Bankhead gave new meaning to the concept of showing her stuff onstage. She was in the play *Dear Charles* by Marc-Gilbert Sauvajon and Frederick Jackson at the Morosco Theatre in 1954 and, during part of the action, sat on a low, padded chair, fluffing her skirt.

Never one to be shy about her body, Bankhead decided to give the first few rows something to remember. She played with her skirts more than ever, lifting them high enough to reveal that she was wearing no underwear.

Three nuns and a priest in the second row immediately left the theater.

3

A Drastic Change of Scenery
(Scenery, Properties, Sound,
and Lighting)

WHEN RED SKELTON played the Paramount Theater for a two-week engagement in New York City, one of his surefire bits was called "Guzzler's Gin," in which he pretended to be a pitchman for gin. He would get progressively drunker as he advertised the smoothness of Guzzler's and then eventually collapse, drunk, on the floor. On the bill with Skelton was Tommy Dorsey and His Orchestra, and one night, one of the musicians added a little something to the supposed gin bottle onstage: two live goldfish.

The audience members in the first couple of rows saw the goldfish before Skelton did and chuckled in anticipation. When he took a huge gulp, Skelton felt the squirming little additions to his drink and knew they were not overly frisky olives. He gagged to prevent himself from swallowing them, as the entire Dorsey band and much of the audience enjoyed the gag.

The final performance at the King's Theatre in Edinburgh, Scotland, featured cowboy performer Roy Rogers. In his act, he included firing pellets from a handgun at saucers tossed into the air.

On this occasion, his hand-eye coordination was somewhat lacking. While shooting, several of the fragments of the saucers struck him, and in the process of trying to avoid the debris, he literally shot Trigger, his horse and longtime companion, directly up the ass.

King Lear had more trouble than just his daughters at a nineteenth-century production of the Bard's tragedy in Washington, D.C. Due to a surplus of cannon balls in the nation's capital, the production decided to use some of the spent ordnance for sound effects in the storm scene. While Lear and the other characters listened to the wind crack and blow, a stagehand would push a wheelbarrow filled with the cannon balls over an uneven surface, simulating the roar of thunder.

This made such an impression on audiences that, one night, the stagehand decided to go for a Category Five hurricane effect. Without authorization, the stagehand dumped the cannonballs out of the wheelbarrow backstage.

Alas and alack, they punched through the flats and came roaring downstage toward the footlights. The "aged" King Lear, spotting the cannon balls barreling toward him, suddenly became as frisky as a puppy, leaping out of their path and creating a storm of laughter from the audience, most of whom could not see the cannon balls.

The great Lillie Langtry was performing the lead in *Camilla* in London. While onstage with her lover, she noticed that the white camellia that she gave him each night in one scene was missing. She subtly acted her way toward the wings and whispered harshly to a stagehand, "My camellia!"

The stagehand responded instantly and, without looking at what she had been given, Langtry approached her paramour, uttering the following, impassioned speech:

"Take this flower, Armand. It is rare, pale, senseless, cold but sensitive as purity itself. Cherish it and its beauty will excel the loveliest flower that grows, but wound it with a single touch and you shall never recall its bloom or wipe away the stain."

With that, she handed him the half-eaten stalk of celery that the stagehand had given her.

Bennet Guillory founded the Robey Theatre in Los Angeles and named it out of admiration for the man who sported that nickname, the great singer, actor, and activist Paul Robeson.

In fact, for many years Guillory toured the one-man show *Paul Robeson* by Phillip Hayes Dean.

The Odyssey Theatre in Los Angeles, now on Sepulveda Boulevard, used to be located nearby on Santa Monica Boulevard. It was there, on a very hot night in 1983, that Guillory was onstage as Robeson with no other accompaniment than blind pianist Howard Smith, when, two minutes before the end of act 1, there was a power failure.

All the lights in the theater went out. It was so dark you could not see your hand in front of your face. Nevertheless, Guillory continued to play Robeson and left the stage, walking off Smith, as was his custom.

By the time they got to the dressing room, the lights had gone back on.

Guillory turned to Smith and told him he had performed the last few minutes of the first act in pitch-black darkness.

"Well, that's not my problem," dryly answered the blind pianist.

Director Michael Arabian liked to stage plays on a grand scale. That is why he secured the backlot of CBS Studio Center in Studio City to stage Euripides' *The Trojan Women.*

Arabian set the play during the first Gulf War. He had all the women wearing black veils and all the men in commando gear. He used the lagoon from the old TV series *Gilligan's Island.* And, after three months of negotiations through a former acting student who was in the reserves, he secured from the Marines an amphibious Humvee vehicle.

The beachhead for the play required 400,000 gallons of water, and the Marines insisted on having one of four different Marines drive the vehicle each time it was used. The Humvee would already be underwater before the audience arrived and took their seats in the bleachers. Then the Humvee would burst out of the lagoon and drive onto the beach. The doors of the Humvee would then open, beach water would pour out, and Menelaus would enter the play.

This never failed to impress audiences, but the impact of one exit of the Humvee was somewhat watered down.

Menelaus, at the end of the play, is intent on killing Helen, but she convinces him to take her back, alive, to Troy.

At this performance, the Humvee would not start. It was meant to drive underwater, and had done so successfully every show. But, as the characters sat in the vehicle waiting to drive back into the water and have the lights go down to end the evening, the Humvee refused to start.

So, thinking on his feet, one of the actors announced, "We've got to walk back." And defying ancient history and the logic that says human beings are not suited to walking back through the ocean to their home, the remaining actors marched off the beach to laughter and then, graciously, applause.

Bill Frenzer was part of the comedy-musical group Ogden Edsl, noted for its hit "Dead Puppies." Ogden Edsl was not above making fun of other kinds of bands, and one night they were performing their punk music song parody "Puke Rock" at the Howard Street Tavern in Omaha, Nebraska.

Frenzer was covered with chains, jangling about the stage while intoning the lyrics: "I am for love and you are for love / But your dad is for hate so let's kill your dad." This warm sentiment was followed by what the band referred to as the "plunger solo," in which Frenzer took a toilet plunger, pretended to play it, and jammed it onto the floor and lifted it up, doing this in a repeated fashion and making a percussion solo.

Unfortunately, on that night, Frenzer plunged into his own hell. The plunger stuck to the floor and he struggled to pull it up with no luck. Using more force, Frenzer suddenly found the plunger's wooden handle zooming up toward his face and pounding into his left eye. Frenzer, reeling, had no idea whether or not he had been permanently blinded, but he continued on with the show. The audience, of course, assumed it was an expertly executed gag.

Afterward, upon closer examination, it was revealed that though his left eyeball was all red, he could see out of it. A nurse friend in attendance took him to Creighton University Hospital, where, while he waited for help, he heard medical professionals down a hallway exclaim, more than once, "He did what?"

One of the most relentless campaigns to make a fellow actor break up laughing onstage took place at the Lyric Theatre in Oklahoma City. Tom Jacobson was playing a carnival barker in the musical *Plain and Fancy,* with music by Albert Hague, lyrics by Arnold Horwitt, and book by Joseph Stein and Will Glickman.

There was a moment in the musical when the entire cast faced Jacobson, their backs to the audience. One night, in an effort to make him burst out laughing, they all stuck their tongues out at the same time. It didn't work.

The next night, during the same moment, the cast smiled at Jacobson en masse; each member had a blacked-out tooth.

Since the play included fresh produce as props, the following night, the cast faced Jacobson with green beans sticking out of their noses. Still Jacobson maintained his composure.

These anarchistic attempts went on for every night of a two-week run, culminating in the strangest gag of all on closing night. When the carnival barker faced the ensemble, each and every cast member stuck out his or her tongue. This time, however, stuck to every tongue was a tiny picture, taken from the program, of Jacobson.

Anton Chekhov famously said that if a gun appears in the first act of a play, it must go off later in the work. Sometimes, it's better if there is no gun at all.

That was the case in the production of Ibsen's *Hedda Gabler* for which Terry Lee ran sound at Carnegie Mellon University in Pittsburgh.

During a climactic scene, the actress playing Hedda, lit in silhouette behind a lace scrim, puts a gun to her head and pulls the trigger. An offstage gunshot is heard and she falls down dead.

Now, many is the story of onstage guns that do not work or that work at the wrong time. But this particular production gave Hedda even more reason to want to kill herself.

On the night in question, Hedda put the gun to her head, and the audience was treated to an awe-inspiring series of clicking noises.

After a long pause, stagehands scrambled around backstage trying to find blanks for the pistol.

An actor, tired of waiting for an entrance, noticed a stool next to the props table and decided to pick it up and bring it down resoundingly on the floor, approximating the sound of a gunshot.

Unfortunately, the stool was of a type often stolen by Carnegie Mellon students and used in their dorms. So, this particular stool had been chained to the table to prevent theft. Hedda patiently held the gun to her head as the sounds of crashing glasses and plates were heard.

The crew burst into laughter at the incongruity of Hedda Gabler waiting to commit suicide with the sound of a Dumpster being upturned. But an onstage actor showed great ingenuity by moving upstage and announcing, in a loud and horrified voice, "Good Lord! Hedda has stabbed herself!"

In keeping with all good theatrical gunshot stories, a blank was found, and immediately after Hedda stabbed herself, she shot herself as well, just to be on the safe side.

Sarah Jessica Parker knows how hard performing on Broadway can be. The critics can rip you apart. Fellow performers can snipe at you. And a scrub brush can alter the way you look.

In fact, during the revival of the musical *Annie* (music by Charles Strouse, book by Thomas Meehan, lyrics by Martin Charnin) at the Alvin Theatre on Broadway, Parker was singing and gesticulating with a scrub brush so inventively that she knocked part of a tooth out of her mouth and somewhere onto the stage.

The name of the song was "It's the Hard-Knock Life."

It is not that unusual to have a piece of scenery break off or fall during a production. What is rare is when that falling piece of scenery is so huge it threatens the lives of any actors near it.

Liam O'Brien was playing the role of Ray, an obnoxious, loud-mouthed youth, in Martin McDonagh's *The Beauty Queen of Leenane*. The Caldwell Theatre in Boca Raton, Florida, had gone to considerable effort in creating the set, a small thatched-roof hut in Ireland. A portion of the roof jutted out from the back wall and extended over the set's kitchen, shelves, and only door. It was an elaborate effort to give a cross-section view of the little house where the action took place.

Ray is an utter jerk, entering and exiting frequently in the course of the evening, always slamming the door. At one point in the story, he enters, hands another character a letter meant for someone else, exits, and then waits ten seconds before bursting into the house again in an effort to catch the character reading the private communication.

One night, Ray nearly got his comeuppance. O'Brien handed over the letter and left the stage, slamming the door ferociously as usual.

But he never got to count to ten.

Upon whipping the door closed, O'Brien was shocked to see a huge section of the thatched roof come crashing down. The audience was, too. It landed one foot behind him and, luckily, made no contact with the other actor. Had it done so, it might have meant "curtains," in more than one sense. For the wooden section that fell was about three feet wide, nearly the length of the stage, and made a terrible sound when it struck the floor.

O'Brien, his heart racing, gathered his wits and reentered what was left of the little house, not to catch his aged scene partner reading the letter but to see if she was in fact still alive.

Not wanting to divert too much from McDonagh's text, he mouthed the words "What the *feck* is going on?"

"Me shelf fell," came the explanation.

"Good-oh," O'Brien replied in a quivering Irish brogue and exited quietly for the first time.

By the time he got offstage, his legs had turned to jelly thanks to this close brush with a permanent closing night.

Leigh Kennicott was present at the production of Molière's *Tartuffe*, done by the theater department at the University of Colorado in Boulder.

The town should have changed its name to "Bolder" that night, for the play was given a Texas theme and set amid a grove of fake trees.

On opening night, Brian Matsuno, playing a minor role, must have been bored in the background. He began to chew the scenery—literally. He began to gnaw on a branch of one of the fake trees, and the audience roared with laughter.

Everyone seemed to love his improvisation—except the two actors playing the lovers, who were supposed to be the focus of the scene, and who probably would have been happy to hang Matsuno from one of the branches of the fake tree.

In 1997, Tony Wheeler was playing Judas in the musical *Jesus Christ Superstar* by Andrew Lloyd Webber and Tim Rice in Kassandra, Greece. Consumed with guilt after turning Jesus in to the authorities,

Wheeler, as Judas, would attach a rope to a hook under the back of his costume and seemingly hang himself for his foul deed.

Unfortunately, one night, the scene became far too real. Wheeler did not properly hook the rope and, with no support, his neck snapped in front of six hundred horrified holiday attendees.

The name of the venue where the accidental death occurred was the Sunny Beach Hotel.

The Rodgers and Hammerstein musical *The Sound of Music* won a Tony Award for best musical of 1959 and ran for 1,443 performances.

The Pioneer Theatre Company's production in Salt Lake City in the 1970s, however, put a new spin on the title song.

As the performers began singing "The hills are alive . . ." the backdrop of the Swiss Alps began to rise from an elevator shaft. Then the Alps got stuck at about knee height and stayed there, suggesting that the song "Climb Every Mountain" should have been renamed "Step Cautiously over Every Mountain."

Not only did the miniature Alps throw the performers off, but they had to contend with carefully walking around the open elevator shaft and not falling to their deaths.

After the end of the first act, the Alps were removed and the hills that had been briefly "alive" were dead for the evening.

Randy Brenner once had to play the Queen's Evil Troll in a production of *Sleeping Beauty.* But that was not the problem.

The Muny in St. Louis, where it was performed, is an enormous space, built around five fully grown oak trees. As the United States' oldest and largest outdoor theater, it can accommodate eleven thousand people. It is so spacious that, in one scene, six players rode out into the playing area on horseback.

For one scene, Brenner would ride out in a full-sized coach pulled by four Shetland ponies, stop center stage, grab Sleeping Beauty (played by then Miss America Susan Powell) and then whisk her off stage right.

One night, the horse trainer gave the Shetland ponies the usual tap to get them to trot to center stage. This time, for some reason, they spooked. They dashed insanely into the playing area, and the coach hooked onto a part of the set—a series of flats with flowers on it, ten to fifteen feet high.

The part of the set that was caught on the coach broke off, causing the coach itself to fall over on its side. Brenner, as the Evil Troll, was now trapped, center stage, in the upended coach because the one door was lying on the ground.

Miss America, as Sleeping Beauty, stared at the accident, shocked, wondering how she was going to be kidnapped.

Brenner, however, took his evil duties quite seriously. He kicked the roof out of the coach, crawled out and got woozily to his feet.

Sleeping Beauty stood stock still, uncertain how the Troll was going to spirit her away in a decimated coach lying on its side. Brenner wondered the same thing and, in a fit of pique, angrily grabbed her by the arm and yanked her away into the wings.

Actors are a remarkable breed. They continue performing even when they are injured, when they feel ill, and, in the case of Alfred Uhry's *The Last Night of Ballyhoo,* when they cannot be seen.

Meredith Hagedorn was ushering at the Canon Theatre in Beverly Hills during the Uhry play when the power went out and the theater was plunged into darkness.

The actors froze onstage. The ushers ran down into the house and carefully began guiding patrons toward the exits with the help of flashlights.

But then, one of the actors onstage came back to life and demanded that everyone stop. Some ushers shone their flashlights on the actor, who called out, "Well, wouldn't you all like to see the end of the show? We've got about fifteen minutes and this is the best part!"

The audience applauded and those standing returned to their seats. The play was finished, thanks to all the ushers shining flashlights on the stage. Each usher held three flashlights: one in each of their hands and one in their mouths.

Sometimes the lights go out unexpectedly, and sometimes the lights come on unexpectedly.

Ronnie Rohrback was the stage manager for Agatha Christie's *Ten Little Indians* at Wheaton Drama Inc. at Wilton Manor in Wheaton, Illinois. This oft-produced murder mystery involves characters getting bumped off, one by one, on an island. During a sequence when the lights were out on the island, the lights also went out at Wilton Manor. A car had smashed into a telephone pole outside.

The enterprising Rohrback figured that even though the lights were supposed to be restored by the end of the play, the audience would accept the rest of the play being done by candlelight. And so, every time another actor made an entrance, it was done with more lit candles.

Fortunately or unfortunately, depending upon your viewpoint, the power came back on a little while later. But the house lights came on during a sequence when the lights were still supposed to be out on Indian Island.

Rohrback quickly ordered the lighting operator to turn off the lights in the house and onstage. The audience thought it was a lightning effect and didn't know what had happened outside until after the show.

Magicians and illusionists have historically performed entertaining bits that seem to threaten their very lives. Then, when they survive the seemingly death-defying act, the audience breathes a sigh of relief and rewards the performer with a burst of applause.

In 1918, one of the world's best illusionists performed a long-standing stunt to close his show. Instead of being greeted with tumultuous applause, he was shot dead and, to this day, it is still unclear whether it was an accident or murder.

At the Wood Green Empire in London, on March 23, 1918, Chung Ling Soo performed his trick "Condemned to Death by the Boxers." It involved assistants firing bullets at Soo, who then used a porcelain plate to catch the bullets. Whenever he performed this illusion, the audience heard the bullets hit the plate and then swirl around on the porcelain. Soo would then step toward the footlights and invite two people from the audience to hold up the dented slugs. Sometimes he awarded the bullets to the volunteers as mementos. Every once in a while, he gave away the plate.

Soo never spoke onstage, but on that night, after the two rifles were fired, his assistants and people in the first couple of rows heard him call out in pain. He took a few steps backward; his knees buckled; and a technician ran onstage, catching him before he fell. It was then that his assistants noticed the dark stain spreading across the front of his robe.

The curtains were drawn, and the stage manager called for the movie screen in the theater to be lowered. A silent newsreel from the War Office was shown. Several minutes later, the film abruptly stopped. The orchestra played "God Save the King," and the two thousand members of the audience left the Wood Green Empire.

Soo's staff, shocked by his death, could neither explain how he did the trick nor why it failed. Magicians around the world, long admirers of Soo, puzzled over the event. The great Harry Houdini wrote to a friend, "There are only two ways it could have happened. One is a failure of exchange . . . or a mixture of bullets." He went on to theorize that if ". . . one of the men, instead of loading the trick cartridge would substitute one of his own . . . that would be murder."

The Iroquois Theater at 24-28 Randolph Street in Chicago was barely a month old on December 30, 1903, when it presented the farce *Mr. Bluebeard Jr.,* starring Eddie Foy, to a packed house. The Beaux Arts–style theater of mahogany and marble had been created by architect Benjamin Marshall and declared "absolutely fireproof," a major consideration because of the fairly frequent theater fires of that era. It had been equipped with an asbestos curtain to separate the audience from any fire that might take place either onstage or backstage.

The Iroquois accommodated 1,724 patrons, but there were 1,900 men, women, and children attending the December 30 holiday matinee, literally standing room only, to see 500 performers grace that grand stage.

Tragically, because regulations were ignored and because of a couple of cruel twists of fate, a fire consumed the interior of the Iroquois that dark day, becoming, for the time, the second most devastating fire in U.S. history.

Foy, dressed in drag and parading about amusingly, had filled the theater with laughter during the first act of the musical comedy. After the intermission, the orchestra began playing "In the Pale Moonlight" and the chorus returned to the stage, singing and dancing. It was about 3:15 P.M.

Huge canvas scenery flats, painted with oil-based paint, were suspended by ropes above the stage. On a catwalk high above the action, stagehand William McMullen noticed a bit of one of the canvas flats brush against a hot reflector behind one of the calcium arc spotlights. A tiny flame erupted and quickly spread.

An on-duty fireman tried to stop the fire, but he was equipped with two tubes of a flame retardant called "Kilfyres" that did nothing to stop the growing conflagration. Below, Foy had just walked onstage for his act 2 entrance when an overhead light shorted out, sparked, and threw flames onto a velvet curtain and flammable props.

When a bit of burning scenery plunged to the stage, the singers fled, but the orchestra played on and Foy did his best to calm the alarmed crowd. In a horrific moment of black comedy, he declared, "Everything is under control," only to watch a huge chunk of burning debris land near his feet. Foy called for the stage manager to lower the asbestos curtain, and this is where bad luck played a huge part in the disaster.

The protective curtain, which could have limited the fire to the stage and backstage area, caught on a protruding light fixture as it was being lowered. Then the wooden tracks jammed, preventing the curtain from moving up or down.

In a panic, the singers and dancers naturally decided to flee the theater from the rear stage door. But that decision sealed the fate of hundreds of people without anyone realizing it. The sudden draft of icy air billowed the flames, which burst past the partially lowered asbestos curtain and into the house. So great was the fireball that it leaped fifty feet across the orchestra seats, all the way to the edge of the balcony. Everything combustible immediately ignited.

"A sort of cyclone came from behind," Foy said later, shakily, "and there seemed to be an explosion."

With the fire now raging throughout the Iroquois and the lights gone, the audience bolted in every direction for the theater's twenty-seven different exits. Here, the lack of adherence to regulations took more lives, as some doors had locked iron gates over them. Some gates were unlocked, but had to be operated by a small lever unfamiliar to most theater patrons of the day. Other doors of the Iroquois opened inward. Many were trampled or crushed against the doors as the surging waves of desperate people struggled to escape.

In darkness, people crawled over bodies piled ten high around the doors and windows, especially those around the stairwell exits in the balcony and on the main floor.

Compounding the terror, a fire broke out just underneath an alley fire escape, prompting people to jump. Those who leaped first were killed on impact. Others landed on dead bodies and survived. The same held true for some who jumped from the balcony to the main floor.

In fifteen minutes, it was all over. There were 572 dead men, women, and children. Later, 27 more would die of injuries, bringing the shocking body count to 602. Among the 500 performers, only the tightrope artist, caught in an area high above the stage with no escape, died.

By the time the fire department arrived, the damage was done. It took them a mere thirty minutes to put out the blaze.

A coroner's inquest was held within a week; more than 200 people testified. A national scandal followed revelations that city inspectors had been given complimentary tickets in order to overlook fire code regulations and let the theater open by its scheduled date. Theater officers, building owners, Chicago Mayor Carter Harrison, and others were indicted.

All the cases were dismissed on technicalities. The only person to actually serve time in jail was a nearby bar owner whose establishment had served as a temporary morgue. He was sentenced for robbing the dead.

Not one injured survivor or relative of the 602 ever received any money in compensation for the disaster.

A new fire code was enacted in Chicago, mandating that all doors in theaters open outward, that exits be clearly marked, and that fire curtains be made of steel. Theater managers had to practice fire drills, as well, with ushers and theater employees.

The Iroquois, which sustained relatively light interior damage, was repaired and reopened a year later as the Colonial Theatre. In 1926, that theater was torn down to make way for the new Oriental Theatre.

The holocaust inside the Iroquois could have been minimized by following regulations, by a functional fire curtain, and by that stage door not being opened at the wrong moment.

But the cruelest irony of all is that the Iroquois Theater fire almost didn't happen. When McMullen, the stagehand, saw the arc spotlight ignite the canvas flat into a small flame, he immediately stretched out on the catwalk to extinguish it with his hands.

It was two inches beyond his reach.

Mjka Scott became an assistant stage manager at the Watford Palace Theatre in Watford, England. She was responsible for far too many jobs during the production of the pantomime of the fairy tale *Jack and the Beanstalk*. One of her duties was to supervise the raising, or flying, of the beanstalk, with the help of an on-duty fireman. One night, she was provided with a replacement fireman, a burly man six feet, six inches tall who clearly would not have any problem pulling on the ropes and raising the beanstalk during their two cues.

There was no counterweight system for the beanstalk, which was made of wooden slats with foot- and toeholds, eight feet long by eighteen inches across. Just to make sure that it was stable, five fifty-pound weights were lashed to the last slat.

But Scott was stunned by the laughter from the audience that accompanied the cue to lift the beanstalk. She looked at the muscular fireman, who was red in the face and had beads of sweat popping out on his forehead. From their position above the stage, Scott looked down at the action below.

Her new assistant, being a man of great strength, had not just added height to the beanstalk. He had uprooted it. The base of the beanstalk and the fifty-pound weights were now swinging dangerously back and forth, threatening to decapitate the actors. They wisely sprawled out on the stage rather than risk having their heads bashed in by a wildly growing beanstalk.

The following night, Scott had a new assistant "learning the ropes."

Dr. Diane Howard is director of performance studies at the University of Mary Hardin-Baylor in Belton, Texas. The play *Lilies of the Field,* based on the book by William E. Barrett, was staged at the university's Hughes Theater. The work was popularized by the film with Sidney Poitier, who played Homer Smith, an ex-GI driving around the Southwest who enlists the aid of some nuns for his overheated car and winds up living with them for a while, building them a chapel. The hilarious and ultimately moving story won Poitier the Oscar in 1963, the first awarded to a black lead actor.

One performance in Belton, however, failed in its attempt at poignancy. The last line was uttered; the curtain was about to fall on a well-performed, timeless classic; lights illuminated the chapel's beautiful stained glass window, made out of gels and representing the show's themes of faith, hope, racial harmony, and companionship.

And then the window fell out onto the stage and the lights went out.

No one associated with the theater is pleased when problems arise with the sets.

Unless, of course, the play is a farce and things go perfectly wrong, thereby improving the show.

Playwright Mark Harvey Levine was attending Carnegie Mellon University when Allen Boretz and John Murray's *Room Service* was produced. Those who recall the 1938 Marx Brothers movie version know how often and how frenetically the characters run in and out of doors.

The last thing you need, in a door-slamming farce, is to have a doorknob fall off ten minutes into the play. But that is exactly what happened one night in Pittsburgh. Miraculously, the actors used it to great comedic effect.

The doors were constructed in such a way that one had to reattach the doorknob in order to open the door. Once the door was closed, the doorknob immediately fell off again.

So, members of the cast began passing the uncooperative doorknob back and forth to each other as needed during the play's first act. A crew member desperately worked to reattach the doorknob, in limited light, during the intermission.

The second act began and the first time the door was slammed—big surprise—the doorknob fell off.

But it got worse—and, as a result, better.

One of the other doors in the set got caught on the carpeting in front of it. The door could only be opened about six inches, and all characters using that door had to squeeze themselves laboriously through the small opening before entering the action.

By the end of the play, characters were either tossing a doorknob back and forth to each other to use on one door or wriggling like worms through the other.

The audience loved it, and Levine, whose short plays have been mounted in more than 100 productions, is convinced it should "normally" be staged that way.

There is an old saying: "To err is human, to forgive divine; but to really screw up, you need a computer."

When *Guys and Dolls* was revived for the fourth time on Broadway, this time at the Martin Beck, the audience found out what can happen when the arts rely too much on computers.

Peter Gallagher, as Sky Masterson, was singing a lovely ballad to Josie de Guzman, as Sarah Brown, when suddenly all the power in the Martin Beck went out. It came back on a couple of seconds later, but the computers immediately reset.

Now, instead of a sweet song of love, Gallagher was being drowned out by the rock-and-roll music of the group Steely Dan, which had played preshow. No one could figure out how to stop the music, so, until the problem was repaired a few minutes later, Gallagher and de Guzman, supposedly in love after all, updated Damon Runyon's characters to modern day and danced to the music of Steely Dan.

John Antony was onstage with Cathy Rigby and others during a touring production of *Annie Get Your Gun,* one that gave a new and controversial interpretation to the title of that musical.

One actress was intent on trying to make Rigby laugh onstage, which is not unheard-of among performers. But Irving Berlin would probably not have signed off on the idea of an actress onstage, full back to the audience, flipping up her skirt toward Rigby to reveal a strap-on dildo attached to her waist.

Antony also recalls that this gun fun resulted in the same performer planting a dildo in the pocket of Rigby's long skirt in place of her gun, so that one night Rigby whipped out the phallus and, for a moment, unknowingly threatened to shoot bullets into the air out of a penis.

There are those who think there is nothing more dramatic onstage than the death of a female character in an opera. Surely there is one thing more overwhelming: the same character dying twice.

When British performer Stella Roman was starring in Puccini's *Tosca,* it was in the libretto that she had to leap to her death from a prison parapet. This was visually accomplished by having her jump from the prison set and land harmlessly offstage on mattresses.

One night, Roman grew concerned that she could injure herself. So she insisted that two extra mattresses be placed on top of the others.

During that historic death, Roman leaped from the parapet, landed on the extra mattresses, and bounced backward into the air and back onto the stage.

She had to climb back up into the prison, in front of the audience, and kill herself all over again.

Melinda Peterson was acting in a college tour of the play *Butterflies Are Free* by Leonard Gershe. She was in the role of Jill Tanner, the wacky actress who develops a deep friendship with a blind man who has been overprotected.

When the tour reached Troy, New York, Peterson was affected by the exceedingly dry weather. Onstage, while performing an intimate scene in a bedroom, she developed a nosebleed that wouldn't stop.

She pluckily went on with the scene, although the audience could clearly see the flow of blood. Finally, a stage manager took pity on her and placed himself behind one of the flats representing the walls of the bedroom, thrust his arm through the wall, and waved some tissues to get her attention.

Despite shattering the reality of the play, Peterson decided to take the tissues and use them to staunch the nosebleed.

The actor playing the blind character had to do some exceptional acting that day; he had to pretend he did not see that arm waving tissues like a white flag through the wall.

The Arts Club Theatre in Vancouver decided to produce Alan Ayckbourn's *Absurd Person Singular* and, due to a rather unsteady set, it became *Absurd People Singular* very quickly on opening night.

The opening scene took place in a kitchen. Susan Wright's character had her head in an oven. She was trying to kill herself. She came very close to doing so.

Things rarely go wrong in the first five seconds of a production. But for this opening, the curtain went up, Wright stuck her head in the oven onstage, and it promptly fell over, right on top of her. Wright was trapped and, because she was rather short, all the audience could now see, while laughing, were her two little legs pumping away furiously.

Margaret Bard, a fellow actress, was herself barely five feet tall. And she took on the Herculean task of trying to lift the oven off of Wright's head. Not only did she fail in her effort, but she found herself also on the floor, kicking with great frustration as she tried to pry Wright's head out.

Finally, a big, strapping member of the audience ruined all the fun by coming onstage, lifting up the oven, and helping Bard and Wright to their feet so that Wright could once again stick her head—more carefully—into the oven.

Nicholas Rice was in the horror parody *Return of the Curse of the Mummy's Revenge,* by James Saar and Joey Miller. Rice was playing the mad, nefarious Dr. Finkelstein. But one night, in Lindsay, Ontario, the joke was on him and it required another doctor's help.

Because his character was basically insane, others kept trying during the show to calm him down. At one point, another character said, "Here, Doc, here's a sedative." Rather than a barbiturate, which would have slowed down the production considerably, Rice would be given a chewable vitamin C tablet. This worked well in rehearsals until one night when he choked on the tablet.

Thereupon Saar, who also directed, found comedic business for Rice so he would not have to eat or swallow the tablet. One time he wore it like a monocle. Another time it went down his pants.

Rice enjoyed the process of finding new things to do with the tablet. But during a preview, he was given, instead of a vitamin C tablet, a Tic Tac breath mint—considerably smaller.

Rice decided to stick it in his ear.

During intermission, he tried to take it out, but it had gone deep into his inner ear. Now Rice had an ache in his ear and had to go back out onstage for act 2 without being able to hear anything out of the ear with a breath mint in it.

The mad doctor had to see a real doctor, who could not reach the mint, and so a hydraulic device sucked it out of Rice's eardrum.

David Gaines was contracted to work one week as a musical director at a Falmouth, Massachusetts, theater presenting *South Pacific.* When he arrived, Gaines was crestfallen to learn he was not conducting an orchestra at all. Instead, his assignment was to hit a bar on a computer at a given moment so that the "virtual orchestra," the orchestra on tape, could play throughout the theater.

Adding insult to injury, Gaines found that the theater was flea-infested. He was constantly scratching himself while he sat jammed in a lighting booth, there to hit a bar to start the music.

During one performance, as he scratched angrily at a flea bite, his arm slipped and he hit the bar, starting the music while performers onstage were in the middle of a conversation. After waiting for the music to stop, and realizing Gaines could not stop it, the actors gamely jumped in, trying to figure out where to start singing along with the song, already in progress.

Gaines finally found a way to stop the music, but the performers, thinking the technical problem would not be repaired for a while, bravely sang on without accompaniment.

The stage manager found a way to get a blackout, even though it was not programmed to happen at that moment. So the actors suddenly found themselves singing in the dark. They decided that the blackout indicated the end of the scene and they stopped singing. In the darkness, they moved to their positions for the next scene.

The lights came up and then Gaines figured out how to get the music started again. The music to "Honey Bun" started once again from the beginning.

Tony Pasqualini was in the cast of Ibsen's powerful drama *Hedda Gabler*, a play that relies on Hedda's offstage death to impact the actors onstage. Unfortunately, during one performance the audience was shown a little bit too much.

The director of the summer stock production had decided that when Hedda runs off to wildly play piano before the gunshot that announces her suicide, her music room should be seen. So there was a gauze curtain hanging in front of her while she sat at the piano. The actress playing Hedda did not actually play piano, so taped music would play until a company apprentice fired a prop gun. Hedda would then, in silhouette, slump dead onto the piano.

One night, the characters Tesman, Hedda's husband, and Judge Brack were talking onstage when Hedda ran off to her music room. She pulled on the curtain to close it and create the silhouette effect. It caught in its tracks and would not close. She desperately tugged at it as the menfolk expressed their concern about her mental state.

The piano music started while Hedda was still yanking at the curtain. She ran to the magical piano, making music by itself, and pantomimed playing it. Her timing had been thrown totally off, and the gunshot went off while she was still pretending to play the piano. Hedda slumped forward, many seconds after being shot, and the play, to everyone's great relief, was over.

Steve Allen and Jayne Meadows agreed to do a summer stock tour of *Tonight at 8:30* for Harold Kennedy. The Noël Coward collection of nine one-acts might have been a bit long for one evening, so they decided to present three, and the tour turned out to be a successful one.

With the exception of poor ticket sales at the theater in the mall in Paramus, New Jersey.

As luck would have it, the Paramus show also saw the tour's greatest moment of unintended humor. Allen, noted for his wit and ability to improvise, had promised Kennedy he would stick to the text. Kennedy was pleased that he had done so for the tour.

But one night, Meadows, who was wearing a sequined gown designed by the legendary designer Edith Head, got up from an onstage sofa and began to cross to another area of the stage. In the process, a black sequined pillow attached itself to her jewel-encrusted behind.

The audience went to pieces, and Meadows was the only one in the theater who did not know why.

Allen could not be asked to let this opportunity go by. As his wife, with a giant, glittering, padded bottom approached him, he warned, "Don't look now, darling, but I think you're being followed."

It is hard to ask a great improviser not to improvise. It may not be that difficult to get a comedic actor to agree to a dramatic role. But in the case of Groucho Marx, the challenge was to change the expectations of his usually adoring audience.

Marx had written the play *Time for Elizabeth* with Norman Krasna, and when Otto Kruger played the lead on Broadway, the production died on the vine.

So, when Harold Kennedy offered to produce the play at the

Grist Mill Playhouse in Andover, New Jersey, Marx agreed. He always felt he, and not Kruger, should have been the lead.

As a gentle drama, *Time for Elizabeth* provided an ideal forum for Marx to show his more dramatic skills. But it turned into *Time for the Old Groucho.* The audience, expecting the madcap machinations for which Groucho and his brothers had become famous, was seriously disappointed. Others were apoplectic, and the reviewers gave it bad Marx.

Groucho told Kennedy, "Well, I've had my fling with Art." Starting with the second performance, he began adding outlandish *shtick* to the otherwise pleasant, unassuming play. By the Saturday matinee, he'd devised a moment in which he pulled a live duck out of a bureau drawer.

When the show continued the tour, the duck went with him. But the serious, dramatic Groucho was long gone.

To producer David Merrick's credit, he exhibited a remarkable grace and humor when the musical *Mata Hari,* based on the World War II spy, went down in flames. In fact, almost every aspect of the show failed during its tryout in Washington, D.C. Perhaps Merrick seemed to be in a good mood because he was giddy with shock.

The show started badly, with a lead actress whom no one had ever heard of, who had no experience. Marisa Mell had good looks, but that was about it. The very first preview was a benefit for the Women's National Democratic Club and First Lady Lady Bird Johnson.

It was enough to kill all federal funding for the arts.

Part of the set collapsed. Several of the dancers stumbled and fell.

Mell herself was caught in the lights half naked as she was trying to change costumes during a blackout.

Making it a disaster of almost biblical proportions was the technical side of the production. In the end, when Mata Hari is to be executed by firing squad, she is brought out on a moving wagon. But the wagon wouldn't move. Mell had to walk onto the stage and prepare to be shot by the firing squad.

Their rifles emitted no sounds. After a moment's hesitation, Mell decided she still had to die and fell to the stage.

As the curtain fell, Mell, not realizing her supposed corpse was still visible to the house, wiped some perspiration off her face.

After it was over, Merrick was spotted standing up in the crowd and generously offering, "Anyone who wants this show for a buck can have it."

Lynn Redgrave made her Broadway debut in a very tricky play, Peter Shaffer's *Black Comedy*. It opens in the dark, with voices heard from the stage. When the show starts, there is a power outage in the house where the play is set, the lights come up onstage and the performers have to act as if they are in the dark.

One would think this clever conceit would not be too hard to understand, especially during the psychedelic year of 1967. But apparently some of the dimmer bulbs in the audience at the Ethel Barrymore were still "in the dark."

To make things clear, the program explained the show's lighting concept. Despite this, and the reviews mentioning same, people regularly lit matches and flashlights in their seats, which forced ushers to tell them the lines delivered in the dark were part of the show.

This lack of comprehension hit a low point at one performance, when Michael Crawford, as the male lead, began his lines in blackness. "There," his voice was heard to say, "how do you think the room looks?"

"Fabulous," came the voice of Redgrave. "I wish you could always have it like this."

"It may look great to you," chimed in a not-too-bright man in the audience, "but we can't see a fucking thing."

4

Noises Off
(Offstage and Outside
the Theater)

PERHAPS THE BEST special effect ever to accompany a Shakespeare play was not even planned. John Gielgud was onstage in the Haymarket Theatre on Suffolk Street in London during World War II. He was already dead, as *Hamlet,* but his departure was made all the more dramatic by a German bomb landing near the theater.

The explosion blew the scene dock doors wide open upstage, and a rush of air blew over the astonished players and first few rows of the audience.

Carl Reiner was part of a Broadway review, *Call Me Mister,* when it was having its out-of-town run in Chicago. Fellow actor Alan Dreeben had bought a secondhand but perfectly maintained Ford for the handsome 1946 sum of $600 and bragged to everyone in the cast each day about how well it ran and how beautiful it looked.

One day, as Reiner was arriving for the matinee from an alley behind the theater, he heard Dreeben's voice, shouting ". . . dirty rotten bastard son of a bitch bastard bastard!" Reiner arrived at the backstage door to hear Dreeben screaming, ". . . should be arrested, shot, and kicked in the balls!"

Suddenly, Reiner heard a splintering sound and, moments later, a block of metal was hurled through the backstage door and smashed to a landing at Reiner's feet. It was a pay telephone.

Dreeben, in a fury, had ripped it from its moorings. Reiner couldn't get Dreeben to say why he was in such a fury, but he convinced him to focus, as they had a show to do.

Later, Betty, Dreeben's wife, told Reiner that she had been on the phone with Dreeben at that moment and had told her husband a kid in their neighborhood had shot his BB gun at the beloved Ford and made a small hole in the windshield.

Reiner wrote a sardonic letter to show producer Herman Levin, asking for additional compensation for "non-contracted work as the company psychiatrist."

Levin agreed and added $35 a week to Reiner's salary.

Pope John Paul II was present for a special performance of the Verdi opera *La Traviata*. What made it particularly special was the greatest series of separate mishaps to occur to performers in the same production on the same night in history.

It all began when lead soprano Andréa Guiot telephoned the theater to say she had the flu and could not go on. Shortly after a replacement was found, baritone Julien Giovanetti called to say he was feeling ill as well. He was not faking it. His wife called thirty minutes later, explaining through tears that Giovanetti had in fact just died of a heart attack.

Contralto Hélia T'Hézan arrived at the theater perfectly healthy, but when she heard the news of Giovanetti's passing, she collapsed in hysterics worthy of any opera star and decided she could not perform that evening, pope or no pope.

Her understudy, Denise Montell, was notified and rushed to the theater, as the audience was now waiting for the belated opera to begin. Montell promptly got ensnarled in a Rome traffic jam, and no one knew when she would arrive.

The theater manager decided the traffic jam, not the death or illnesses, was a clear indication that the show must *not* go on and suggested that *La Traviata* be canceled because it was jinxed.

"Jinxed? Pah! Jinxed!" exclaimed lead tenor Alexandre Mazota. He insisted on the performance going ahead, and, striding onstage confidently, he fell through a trap door, broke his leg, and had to be carried out of this miraculous papal performance on a stretcher.

The play *Oh! Calcutta!* was heralded for its nudity when it was first performed in the United States.

Apparently, other cultures are more at ease with the idea of nakedness onstage. On the play's opening night in Stockholm, Sweden, three separate couples showed up with their tickets—and without clothes. The house manager threw them out.

One of the unhappy nude patrons explained, "We understood you had to be nude to get in."

Noted for his daring performances at the Los Angeles theater company Evidence Room, director and cofounder Bart DeLorenzo found himself in the middle of a dangerous and weird offstage performance during the run of *Don Carlos* by Friedrich Schiller.

The house was full that night, thanks in part to the attendance of twenty or more students from California State University, Los Angeles. Well after the play had started, however, DeLorenzo heard the metallic front door of the theater bang noisily.

Leaving the theater, he entered the spacious lobby of the Evidence Room to see a punkish woman in her twenties with spiked hair and a purse made out of a coconut. She spoke loudly and DeLorenzo had to hush her a couple of times. She began to look for money to buy a ticket, and her loud voice forced DeLorenzo to take her into his office so she would not be heard in the theater.

The young woman with questionable manners and fashion sense then declared she did not have any money, hoping DeLorenzo would let her in for free. He suggested she use a credit card. She opened her coconut wider, claiming she did not have one. DeLorenzo easily spotted her Visa credit card and suggested she use it.

When they were back in the lobby, DeLorenzo had to quiet the woman again. He handed her back the card and decided not to run the credit card machine until intermission, again for fear it would distract the audience and performers. He whispered this explanation to the woman, who did not seem to understand and loudly shouted "What?" a couple of times.

Officially giving up, DeLorenzo took the interloper by the elbow and tried to usher her outside. She struggled to free herself from his hold but he succeeded in getting her outside the Evidence Room.

"You're not going to let me in!" the young woman suddenly, perceptively realized.

"No," said DeLorenzo, struggling to keep his temper in check. "Come back some other night."

With no warning, the woman hauled off and smacked him in the head with her coconut purse.

"I can't believe you did that!" exclaimed DeLorenzo, holding his face. He saw her attempting a follow-up shot and grabbed the hand holding her purse. She dislodged it by bending back DeLorenzo's thumb until the pain forced him to let go of her hand.

Then, impulsively, she turned and dashed across busy Beverly Boulevard, nearly getting hit by a passing car in the process.

She looked back over her shoulder, still in the middle of the busy thoroughfare, and shouted, "I'm going to bring my brother back and he's going to kill you!"

Ken Ruta has played many leading roles for the Guthrie Theater since 1963. But his debut in that year was less than auspicious.

Cast as The Ghost and Second Gravedigger in *Hamlet*, he was performing with the likes of Jessica Tandy, Hume Cronyn, George Grizzard, and Zoe Caldwell. There was a window in the back wall of the theater in those days, and Tyrone Guthrie decided that, for the bows, it would be interesting to have Ruta, as The Ghost, watch the proceedings from that window.

This would have been fine, but on opening night, as the applause began, Ruta climbed up the ladder toward the window only to find that it was already occupied by a photographer from *Life* magazine.

"It's my curtain call!" Ruta hissed angrily.

"Get the hell out of my way!" spat the photographer, who kept shooting and kept Ruta from his first curtain call at the Guthrie Theater.

I Know My Love was the name of a play that Lynn Fontanne and Alfred Lunt toured in 1950–51. In fact, they did not know what awaited them.

The seemingly endless string of disasters began in Hartford, Connecticut, where there was a robbery backstage. The prop man's wife was knocked down in the street outside. When the production moved on to the town of Springfield, things got no better. Esther Mitchell, playing a maid, got a brain concussion when a prop box fell on her head.

In Portland, Maine, Fontanne tripped on the hem of her dress while coming out of her hotel, fell, and broke her arm. Lunt was so stunned and upset that he ran off in a panic. Using a scarf to support her arm, Fontanne found her way to a local doctor, who gave her, appropriately, a local anesthetic, and she wore her arm in a sling onstage that night. Lunt apologized, humiliated, for his bad behavior.

Could it get any worse? By all means. Pittsburgh was inundated with thirty inches of snow, stopping the show and costing the producers thousands of dollars. Lunt and Fontanne's car was snow-bound for a week. Detroit was next, and the train they took crawled at an agonizing pace during the harsh winter. The scenery, costumes, makeup, and properties did not arrive in time for the opening.

Then, it was off to Cleveland, where Fontanne's real-life maid, Alma, fell seriously ill and had to be sent home. Cincinnati had a blizzard. Dayton topped Cincy by providing an ice storm . . . and a railroad strike. The scenery went from Columbus to Toledo by truck while the company had to travel by bus.

By the time they finally arrived in Washington, D.C., Lunt and Fontanne learned that their dear friend Ivor Novello had died.

The sentence "They really brought down the house" usually implies a strong and positive reaction from the audience. However, when, on May 15, 2004, *When Harry Met Sally* (adapted from the film by Marcy Kahan) was being performed at the Theatre Royal Haymarket in the West End, they *really* brought down the house, and while it was a strong reaction, it was not necessarily positive.

Kevin Collins was onstage doing a quiet, intimate scene with Alyson Hannigan and Elizabeth Jasicki when the chandelier over the seats suddenly came loose and rained down chunks of plaster cherubs on the heads of unsuspecting spectators.

The chandelier itself fell four feet before it was held in place by a safety chain. But the plaster bombardment sent fifteen people to the hospital for treatment. Star Luke Perry came out into the audience and helped direct audience members out of the theater. Two performances were missed while fire crews repaired the ceiling of the Haymarket.

Maybe chandeliers in theaters should be outlawed.

When the musical *The Phantom of the Opera* opened in 1988, no one knew it would compete with *Cats* as the only Broadway show to run past seven thousand performances.

In the beginning, none of the audience members knew, either, that a chandelier, as a special effect, would come plummeting down from the ceiling of the Majestic Theatre, stopping just short of landing on the patrons' heads.

Early on in the run, one man had a heart attack and died, thinking the chandelier was actually going to land on him. Paramedics arrived on the scene and carted away the unfortunate theatergoer, and the musical had to be restarted.

When director Richmond Shepard was working for the Los Angeles Civic Light Opera's Musical Theatre Workshop, teaching Mime and Musical Theater Performance, a very large-scale production of *Gone With the Wind* was going on in the Dorothy Chandler Pavilion.

Pernell Roberts and Lesley Ann Warren were in the roles of Rhett and Scarlet. Shepard, sitting in the middle of the orchestra section, was dazzled by the sequence depicting the burning of Atlanta, with flames blasting through the buildings upstage.

Roberts led a wagon, pulled by a live horse, onto the immense stage. Warren, by his side, joined Roberts in taking in the enormity of the conflagration. They said an emotional farewell to each other. Roberts exited stage right and Warren, leading the horse and wagon, exited stage left.

Once Roberts was offstage, he must have assumed that his microphone was off. But his voice, lowered as he spoke to a stagehand, was clearly audible.

He said, "She's scared shitless of that horse."

Three thousand people laughed, while Atlanta burned.

If a performer could only know in advance that something was about to go wrong, it might be used to strengthen the show.

Magician Gerry Katzman was once performing outside during the Los Feliz street fair in Los Angeles. As he prepared for his final trick, he noticed a huge cluster of balloons floating by, unseen by his audience. He assumed they had come loose from a vendor's stand and proceeded to introduce his next act, known as "The Cup of Doom."

Within the huge crowd, a burly, big-mouthed man called out, "Why's it called 'The Cup of Doom'?"

The audience laughed but Katzman refused to respond to the challenge. He was not about to give away the trick, in which a cup he raised over his head would be smashed down upon a table in front of him and disappear from sight.

Speaking of disappearing from sight, as Katzman raised the cup over his head, preparing for his finale, he noticed, out of the corner of his eye, the bouquet of balloons was now headed for the power station that supplied electricity to a large portion of eastern Los Angeles.

Realizing the crowd did not know this, Katzman hesitated for dramatic effect, as the balloons rapidly approached an exposed transformer. Then, with impeccable timing, he slammed the cup down on the table. As the cup disappeared from sight, the balloons hit the transformer and created a huge, rattling sonic boom. It shook the entire neighborhood, and everything running on electricity suddenly stopped.

The audience jumped, looked around, and then turned back, awestruck, to Katzman.

"*That's* why it's called 'The Cup of Doom,'" smiled Katzman, and took a bow.

The incomparable escape artist and magician Harry Houdini (Ehrich Weiss) defied death during feats such as manacled bridge jumps, escaping from a box while underwater, and remaining in an airtight bronze coffin for one and a half hours. It is the cruelest of ironies that he died of a freak accident.

Houdini was in Montreal, where he had lectured on spiritualism, which he debunked whenever possible. He had recently broken an ankle and was reclining in his dressing room at the Princess Theatre, speaking with some McGill University students.

Enter Wallace Whitehead, known as Gordon, a divinity student, who asked Houdini if he could absorb punches to the stomach. "Would you mind if I delivered a few blows to your abdomen?"

Houdini, not one to back down from a challenge, began to raise himself up from the pillows supporting him on his seat. Whitehead, not waiting for Houdini to rise or even stiffen his stomach muscles, delivered four or five blows to his abdomen while standing over him.

"Hey, there, you must be crazy! What are you doing?" Houdini cried out. Whitehead ceased his attack. "That will do," Houdini admonished him.

Tragically, that's what did him in. The punches were delivered on October 22, 1926. Houdini continued with his performance schedule though he was starting to feel unwell.

By the time he checked into Grace Hospital in Detroit, it was too late. His appendix had been ruptured by Whitehead's blows.

Harry Houdini, who had so amazed the world with his tricks and escapes, who did not believe in the spirit world although he desperately tried to contact his beloved dead mother, died on October 31, 1926, Halloween.

Janet Waldo Lee, widow of Robert E. Lee, writing partner of Jerome Lawrence, was present for not only the memorable opening nights of this famous team, but also the nerve-wracking behavior of performers both backstage and offstage.

For example, when Rosalind Russell was cast to play the lead in Lawrence and Lee's *Auntie Mame* at the Broadhurst, she began a long series of contract negotiations that never got resolved during rehearsals. She actually signed the contract just before curtain on opening night.

When Paul Muni played Henry Drummond in the courtroom classic *Inherit the Wind* at the National on Broadway, his insecurity was so great, he literally told Bob Lee, before going onstage that first night, "I'll give you a million dollars if you'll go on for me."

Despite Muni's reputation as a fine actor and the recognition he received for the play, he constantly fiddled with his appearance without consulting anyone. Waldo Lee recalls that on some nights he wore a huge nose or new makeup, or no makeup at all.

When Lawrence and Lee came backstage one night, as they

customarily did, to congratulate him on that evening's performance, Muni yelled "No!" and asked them to stop coming backstage, because he was not doing their work justice and it made him nervous.

The next night they complied, and Muni told his wife, Bella, "Tonight, it was so bad, the boys didn't even come back."

Steve Feinberg found a charming, intimate theater in Hollywood for the production of his play *A Nervous Little Magazine*. While that Falcon Theatre no longer exists (there is a Falcon in Burbank), it clearly had an old Hollywood charm, with a rose garden outside and handprints from legendary players such as John Barrymore, Basil Rathbone, and Errol Flynn imbedded in the walkway.

The owner, Ralph Faulkner, was well into his nineties and blind in one eye; he could see only a few feet in front of him in the other. He walked with the aid of two canes and barely subsisted on the money he made booking the theater.

Faulkner had charmed Feinberg with tales of his old Hollywood job as a fencing coach. Faulkner had in fact choreographed the famous fight scene on the staircase between the Sheriff of Nottingham and Robin Hood (Rathbone and Flynn) in the classic film *Robin Hood*.

So it is not surprising that Feinberg agreed to book the Falcon. On a balmy, pleasant August night, *A Nervous Little Magazine* was scheduled to open in front of a sold-out house.

Thirty minutes before the doors of the Falcon opened, however, Faulkner admitted to Feinberg that a small detail had slipped his aged mind: he had booked a Mexican wedding in the four-thousand-square-foot studio right next door to the theater.

So, as the patrons for Feinberg's play began to arrive, so did five hundred guests for the Mexican wedding, along with several mariachi bands and the bride and groom, who entered the garden next to the theater and studio on a flower-covered cart, pulled by two donkeys with fur dyed white for the occasion.

As the donkey cart was unloaded behind the theater, Feinberg, alone with his thoughts, got tears in his eyes, and not because he was easily moved at weddings. He punched a panel of old scenery from a production of *Richard III* and felt, akin to Shakespeare's character, how unfair life could be.

But after staring into Faulkner's apologetic, partially blind, cataract-filled eyes, Feinberg felt compassion for him and assured the theater owner it would be all right.

Which, of course, it wouldn't. The audience for the play had to wend its way through the wedding guests, slowly, laboriously.

Inside the theater, as the play began, so did the mariachi music outside, and the guitars, horns, and singing drowned out a large portion of the dialogue for the evening. At one particularly potent moment in *A Nervous Little Magazine*, about the start-up of a magazine, a character fears something has happened to his wife when she doesn't answer the phone.

In the moment when he wonders whether his wife is alive or dead, a donkey outside hee-hawed and shattered the drama, sending the audience, and Feinberg, in the wings, into gales of laughter.

When the play, thankfully only ninety minutes long without intermission, was over, the audience was surprisingly upbeat and pleasant. A few actually mingled at the wedding outside and had some food, welcomed by the father of the bride.

All the critics in attendance mentioned the wedding reception with amused delight, and were generally supportive of the cast for their tenacity and focus. In all the reviews of *A Nervous Little Magazine,* no one, and certainly not Ralph Faulkner, was blamed for the wedding that rendered the play incomprehensible.

Tony-winning producer Hal Luftig was present when an April Fool's Day trick was pulled on the audience during the run of Ariel Dorfman's *Death and the Maiden.* Unfortunately, the trick backfired.

Stars Glenn Close, Richard Dreyfuss, and Gene Hackman decided to tease the audience, clearly interested in seeing so much star power on the same stage. During the April 1 show, as the lights went down in the Brooks Atkinson, an announcement was heard: "Ladies and gentleman, Ms. Close, Mr. Hackman, and Mr. Dreyfuss will be unable to appear." It was a three-character play.

Chaos broke out. Patrons charged toward the exits to storm the box office and demand refunds. The box office, usually notified of such an event beforehand, had no idea what was going on and denied that there were understudies going on for the three actors.

After sixty seconds of raised voices and scurrying audience members, Glenn Close's voice was heard throughout the theater: "Ladies and gentlemen, we're all here. April Fool's!"

While most of the audience laughed and began to relax, many theatergoers were already in the lobby and had to be convinced by ushers that it was all a joke and that Close, Dreyfuss, and Hackman would indeed appear, even though it had been announced that they wouldn't.

Some disgusted patrons had actually left the theater, thinking three understudies were going on. They could not be found before the play began.

The performance started fifteen minutes late and there was much amused laughter throughout, even though Chilean playwright Dorfman's play was a powerful and harrowing indictment of citizens tortured under a dictatorship.

Stage managers are responsible for many tasks in live theater. But one terrible night in Lake Worth, Florida, Melanie McPherson suddenly became responsible for keeping a show running while trying to save two lives.

The Lake Worth Playhouse was staging the musical *Kiss Me Kate* (book by Sam and Bella Spewack, and music and lyrics by Cole Porter). To open the show, all four leads were onstage and director Barbara Musgrave had the ten or so members of the ensemble enter through the house. They did this by walking out the stage door, down an alley, onto the sidewalk in front of the theater, and through the lobby into the house, accompanied by McPherson.

One night, just before the start of the show, McPherson felt the building shudder slightly. She had no time to investigate, however, as she led the ensemble outside and down the alley.

But as they reached the front of the Lake Worth Playhouse, they were horrified to see that a pickup truck had jumped the curb on Lake Avenue, struck two elderly people, and smashed into the front of the theater. McPherson, who happened to be a nurse, ordered the actors to continue with the show. She ran inside and told the lighting operator to handle stage manager duties and then returned outside to perform mouth-to-mouth resuscitation on the two bleeding victims.

The elderly couple was taken away in an ambulance and McPherson reentered the theater. She quickly washed off her blood-covered face and resumed her stage manager duties. Backstage, the leads, according to actor Doug Cooney, could see the shocked expressions on the faces of the ensemble members and asked what had happened. They were not told, in an effort to deliver the best possible show.

The four men in the pickup truck, according to Musgrave, had glassy eyes and appeared to be on drugs. They were never charged with any crime. Despite McPherson's heroic efforts, the two older pedestrians died.

The audience knew nothing about it until after the show was over.

Bill Rauch is a founding member of the Cornerstone Theater Company, a unique troupe that uses both professional and nonprofessional actors in locations that address issues of those local communities.

It was during the staging of *The Pretty Much True Story of Dinwiddie County* that founding member and actor Amy Brenneman, now firmly established in TV and film, had to question why she did theater at all.

In rural Dinwiddie, Virginia, Cornerstone had set up a temporary dressing room, made out of black plastic, behind the outdoor stage where the show was being performed. One day, Brenneman found feces on the ground inside the makeshift dressing room. She told the stage manager, who cleaned it up, that she suspected an animal had crawled into the plastic tent.

The next day, however, Brenneman found a new crop of solid waste material. Again, the stage manager was summoned. Brenneman was beginning to feel a bit uneasy about working in Dinwiddie.

The third day in a row, Brenneman found not only fecal material but, revealingly, a roll of toilet paper.

It was discovered that an unknown local cast member had thought the black plastic tent was an outdoor bathroom.

It is arguable that the most exciting venue for live theater is not in a theater at all. Site-specific theater was the instigator of a very memorable interaction for actress Linda Castro, one that, rather than involving an audience member, involved innocent persons on the street.

The play was Naomi Iizuka's experimental work *Carthage: Fire.* It was the beginning of a cycle of plays about ancient Greek mythology and told the tale of doomed lovers Dido and Aeneas. As their punishment, they are splintered like shards of glass and sent to live in our contemporary world.

As if the premise were not interesting enough, director Lisa Portes of Theatre E! had the production take place in a gutted building in San Diego. The Architectural Arts building on F and Thirteenth streets was as tall inside as a warehouse, and at one point, an actor sat on a swing suspended from the towering ceiling.

As if the venue were not interesting enough, Castro was playing the role of a man going through a sex-change operation while working as an exotic dancer. So she was in fact a woman playing a man becoming a woman. The costumer padded her groin area to suggest she was not quite yet all woman.

As if the role were not interesting enough, the play required Castro, who was playing more than one role in *Carthage: Fire,* to change one costume quickly, run outside the building and sprint two blocks to get to the other side of the enormous building and make a different entrance.

Theatre E! supplied Castro with a person to run along with her to provide help and protection should she need it. One reason she might was her costume. It was unbelievably skimpy, and included thigh-high boots and a feather boa.

One night, as Castro and the crew member dashed down the street outside the Architectural Arts building, they were joined by two men running alongside them. The men were clearly homeless and smelled of urine and alcohol, but meant no harm. One had a bandaged head and the other had a bandaged hand. They were otherwise in good shape and easily kept up, running along with Castro and her companion.

"What's going down, man?" one homeless man asked.

"Nothing," replied the crew member. "We're just in a hurry."

"Something's going down!" the homeless man told his friend, smiling, anxious to find out. They kept running with them.

"Are the cops after you?"

"We know a good place to hide!"

As they all arrived at the entrance to the building, the two homeless men were told Castro was part of a play. They grew somber, thoughtful and then asked if they could watch.

Castro agreed and gave them specific instructions how to enter the scene. The homeless men agreed and, good to their word, entered with Castro into the play and became silent parts of the set.

With a play like *Carthage: Fire*, it is no surprise that the audience assumed they were actors dressed as vagrants.

When the play was over, they exited without a word.

Do Patent Leather Shoes Really Reflect Up? is a musical play by John Powers about the trials and tribulations of life in a 1950s Catholic school. At the community theater in Geauga, Ohio, Stacy Burris learned just how tough life in the 1950s could be.

Burris played a secretary in the opening scene, then dashed off-stage to be costumed by a battery of dressers to reenter moments later as a nun during the first song. This was accomplished by one person in the costuming assembly line helping Burris change her dress, a second putting the nun's habit on her, while a third helped secure a veil on top of her head. The last in line was a fellow actress who pinned the veil in place. And then out Burris dashed for the musical number. This quick change ran like clockwork during rehearsals—but not, of course, on opening night.

Burris delivered her lines as the secretary, came offstage, got out of the dress, had the habit and veil put on; for the finishing touch, the actress took the straight pin, missed the veil, plunged it into Burris's scalp, and moved on to her next task.

Burris resolutely went out and danced and sang while a thin trickle of blood slowly coursed down her face.

The next time Burris was offstage, she cornered the perpetrator and hoarsely whispered, "Get it out! Get it out!" Burris had previously complained about the tightness of the veil, so the fellow actress assumed that was the problem. She wiggled the veil a bit, good-naturedly whacked Burris on the back of the head, needled her in a different way by telling her to stop being such a baby, and walked off.

Burris felt that she was in some alternate universe of pain as she approached distracted people backstage, barking in a whisper, "Someone, get it out! Needle! Needle!"

Everyone assumed she was complaining about the tightness of the veil, saying it hurt like a needle, and ignored her pleas for help.

Finally, the actress who had plunged the needle in her scalp understood what had happened and took it out. There are many stories of Catholic school cruelty, but rarely do they involve the punishment of a nun.

The audience usually sees costumed actors onstage or in dressing rooms. But during the collection of one-acts known as *Stop, You're Killing Me* by James Leo Herlihy, author of *Midnight Cowboy*, they had the chance to observe a curious performance in the lobby.

It was at the Dobama Theatre in Cleveland Heights, Ohio, where a few of the actors were planted in the audience. They entered the third play from their seats.

Howard Margulis, a short, impish actor, went into the lobby during every intermission, and, like a silent film comedian, played the same gag every time. The Dobama at that time had a number of attractive pottery pieces for sale in the lobby. Margulis, wearing a long raincoat as part of his costume, always caught the attention of the milling theatergoers.

Every night, he planted a Hershey's chocolate kiss inside a pottery jar prior to the theater opening. Then, at intermission, he would wait until there was a large group of people browsing. He would then worm his way to the front, remove the lid of the jar in question, pluck out the piece of chocolate, hold it in the air for a moment so everyone could see it, and then unwrap it, pop it with great pleasure into his mouth, and walk away.

He would then have the satisfaction, as he retreated, of seeing the patrons, night after night, opening the lids of all the empty pottery jars, looking futilely for another piece of candy.

In 1986, a group of prisoners in Sweden was cast in a production of Samuel Beckett's seminal work of absurdist theater, *Waiting for Godot.* Jan Jonson, the director, was following in the footsteps of Rick Cluchey, who had done the same while an inmate. Cluchey had also founded the San Quentin Drama Workshop, and was eventually pardoned by Governor Jerry Brown of California for his work with prisoners and the dramatic form.

Jonson had arranged not for a single performance of *Godot*, but for an entire Swedish tour, and all sixteen thousand tickets immediately sold out. The five inmates chosen out of 1,400 in Kumla Prison, 125 miles west of Stockholm, were transported to the site of the first performance in Gothenburg's City Theatre. They spent the night in the local prison and then, the next day at eleven o'clock, while the lighting was finalized, the prisoner-actors were sent for from the dressing room.

They were not to be found. After lunch, a radio interviewer in Gothenburg approached Jonson and asked about the rumor the prisoners had disappeared. Jonson explained they were rehearsing in the attic.

But the Kumla prison director, accompanying the tour, decided at six in the evening to send out a national alert. Landvetter Airport, the train station, restaurants, and other areas were being watched.

At seven o'clock, the scheduled time for the curtain, Jonson knew the play would never be performed. Rafael, the only prisoner who had not run away, was furious. He went to the dressing room and laid down, waiting to go back "home" to Kumla.

At five minutes after seven, Jonson took the stage, with a bottle of mineral water and a rickety wooden chair. He explained to a stunned audience that four of the five performers were not in the building. For two hours, Jonson remained on stage, discussing the production concept, the rehearsal process, and the first time he had met Beckett.

After the theater had emptied, Rafael said good-bye to his wife, and other relatives of the prisoners stood around, crying. But the prisoner who'd stayed was allowed to spend that one night with his wife in a Gothenburg hotel, with the bill sent to the Swedish government. In the morning, he went back to Kumla.

Newspapers in Europe were filled with reports of the escaped convict-actors and the sold-out tour of *Waiting for Godot* that never took place.

Cluchey, who had instigated the idea of prisoners doing *Godot* in the first place, received a clipping of one of the stories. It had been sent by Samuel Beckett in Paris.

Attached was a small note. It simply read, "I guess they couldn't wait."

Brooke Shields found out just how hard working on Broadway could be when she played the part of Rizzo in the musical *Grease!*

Dying of thirst after a musical number, she had a moment offstage and spied a cup of water. She quickly gulped it down—but it turned out to be hydrogen peroxide, which is much better at cleaning cuts than quenching thirst.

Shields missed the second act of the show and spent the entire night throwing up.

Most disasters in the theater occur due to fire or an accident. But one of the most horrific events in the history of live theater occurred in Moscow. It was due to a word that we are forced to hear constantly in the modern age: terrorism.

On October 23, 2002, the very popular musical *Nord-Ost* was being performed in the Dubrovka Theatre in the southern outskirts of Moscow. At about 9 P.M., an explosion and gunfire were heard outside the theater. About 42 rebels from the republic of Chechnya, where violence had raged for years in a battle for independence from Russia, burst into the Dubrovka. The rebels, including women guerrillas with explosives strapped to their bodies, took 900 people hostage, including 90 members of the theater staff.

After releasing a few hostages, the rebels demanded that Russian military forces be removed from Chechnya. They threatened to blow up the building if a counterattack was launched upon the theater.

Freed hostages also said that the Chechen rebels would release the children hostages if the rebels could communicate with the media. At midnight, the NTV television network broadcast statements from both hostages and rebels. Later, two Chechen representatives from Russia's parliament, other Duma leaders—including reformist Irina Khakamada and popular singer Iosif Kobzon—all tried to mediate with the rebels, to no effect.

The standoff sparked antiwar protests in Moscow, urging President Vladimir Putin to meet the demands of the rebels.

At about five o'clock in the morning on the third day of the hostage crisis, Russian Special Forces, which had promised not to storm the building unless they were notified that hostages were being killed, attacked. It was later claimed that they had received word that hostages were in fact being killed by the rebels.

The Special Forces, once inside the Dubrovka, used a disabling gas that was not identified. In the ensuing shootout, all the rebels were killed.

But about 129 hostages also died. All but two of them succumbed to the gas used by the Special Forces. More than sixty lawsuits were filed against the government and its handling of the hostage crisis. The Chechens, before the siege, had released 200 women, children, and Muslim hostages.

In 2004, *Izvestia,* the Moscow daily, reported that Chechen-born Ruslan Elmurzayev, who headed the economic security service at Moscow's PrimaBank, had financed the assault on the Dubrovka.

Nord-Ost was a lighthearted musical about the history of Russia.

It was opening weekend of Stephen Sondheim's *Follies,* performed by the Palo Alto (California) Players at the Lucie Stern Theatre. An offstage singer, hired just for that weekend, was bored between songs. He called a local Domino's pizza parlor and ordered a pizza to be delivered to the Palo Alto Players' greenroom, on the side of the building.

The backstage area was jammed, and the women with headdresses and big costumes actually went outside the building to make their entrances out of the stage right door, which was left uncharacteristically unlocked.

That night, Peter Bliznick and Toni Tomei were singing a tender duet, "Too Many Mornings," when four hundred people saw a young Domino's pizza delivery man walk through the open stage door onto the stage and stare at the singers and then at the audience, transfixed by his theatrical premiere.

The pizza delivery man stepped backward, as if he'd come face to face with some nightmarish vision, exited the building, and found the greenroom, delivering the pizza as ordered.

Bliznick and Tomei were so into their moment onstage, they never noticed anything wrong, except the audience laughing, for the very first time, during their love ballad.

Opening nights can be quite thrilling. Sometimes, the electricity of the moment can even make the audience a little dazed and confused.

During the opening of *Cats* on Broadway, a show that must have made an impression on someone, since it ran for eighteen years at the Winter Garden, performer Ann Miller ran into newspaper columnist Earl Wilson.

Giddy with the energy of the evening, Miller kidded, "You know what? I'm going to open a show across the street called *Dogs*."

Never kid a newspaper columnist. The next day, Wilson wrote in the *New York Post*, "*Ann Miller wants to open a show called Dogs.*"

The true, unsung hero of live stage is the stage manager, who often solves the impossible without the audience even knowing there is a problem.

Jerry Stiller was in Terrence McNally's comedy *The Ritz* at the Longacre in 1975. He played amusing tough guy Carmine Vespucci. Among the props he had in the dressing room, prior to coming onstage one night, were a mink coat and a mock .38 caliber pistol.

During one performance, Stiller went into the dressing room to grab the coat and gun, only to find them gone. Someone had clearly walked by the theater, reached through the iron bars over the window, and snagged both items.

Panic-stricken, Stiller found stage manager Larry Ford and told him of the crisis. "What do I do? I can't go on without my gun!"

Ford handed Stiller his stage manager script decisively and promised to be back quickly.

Stiller paced back and forth, agonizing, for five minutes.

Good to his word, Ford returned with another mink coat and another gun, also very realistic in appearance.

Stiller was flooded with relief and took both items, readying himself for his entrance. He asked Ford where he'd gotten them so fast.

"I borrowed the coat from a lady in the audience," said the intrepid stage manager. "The gun I got from a cop on Forty-eighth Street. Now go ahead. Do your scene."

Playwright John Osborne was an assistant stage manager before he helped revolutionize modern British drama with his *Look Back in Anger*. In those times, the call boy would knock on the doors of players to indicate "half hour," "quarter hour," "five minutes," and "beginners."

But Osborne found himself in a company with no call boy. He would knock on the door of one particular performer, Miss Atkins, who would always ignore his knocks and make him worry that she hadn't heard him. He would always have to knock additional times before Atkins would begrudgingly call out, through the closed door, that she had heard him.

One performance, in the Hippodrome Theatre, Osborne knocked and Atkins did not reply. With curtain time approaching, he whipped open the door in anger, only to find Miss Atkins in the process of inserting a sanitary napkin.

Atkins never ignored his knock on the door after that.

One of the greatest opening nights in Broadway history, August 25, 1980, is also one of its saddest.

The musical *42nd Street,* helmed by the great choreographer and director Gower Champion, opened at the Winter Garden that night at 6:45. By the time it was over, the audience was on its feet and gave the show eleven curtain calls.

Producer David Merrick, a public relations wizard, appeared onstage for a curtain speech, something he usually never did. Merrick, his hand on his chin, looked down as the applause finally died down.

"This is a very tragic moment," Merrick said, not smiling.

The audience exploded in laughter.

"No, no, no, no, you don't understand," Merrick protested. "I have to tell you, Gower Champion is dead."

Champion had died earlier that day from a rare blood disease. Merrick, not wanting the news to affect the cast, including Champion's girlfriend, Wanda Richert, playing the lead, had kept the company in rehearsals all day. Telephone communications were cut off. The hospital where Champion died was sworn to secrecy.

After Merrick finished his curtain speech, it seemed the shock was so great, after such a triumphant production, that no one could move. Actor Jerry Orbach, observing Merrick's and the Winter

Garden crowd's immobility, ordered the curtain to come down, the cast to leave the stage, and the audience to vacate the theater.

42nd Street, with music by Harry Warren and lyrics by Al Dubin, played from 1980 to 1989 at three different theaters on Broadway, for a total of 3,486 performances.

Sir John Gielgud recalled being in the play *The Chiltern Hundreds* by William Douglas Home. One of the performers, A. E. Matthews, was in the habit of sleeping in his dressing room. One day, the call boy found Matthews lying on the floor.

In great terror, the boy ran to the stage manager and told him, "Mr. Matthews is dead!"

Before anything could be done, Matthews himself strolled into the backstage area and prepared to go on.

After that performance, Matthews took the boy aside and said, "Next time you find me on the floor, I suggest you tell them, 'I *think* Mr. Matthews is dead.'"

Due to the close quarters of performers during the run of a play, great friendships can be born. Great alliances can be forged. Great enemies can be made. But the woman known as the First Lady of the Theater in the United States actually received a marriage proposal during the first act of a play.

Helen Hayes was madly in love with Charles MacArthur, who, along with his writing partner Ben Hecht, had their play *The Front Page* open in 1928 at the Times Square Theatre. She knew that

MacArthur could not afford to marry her unless the play was a hit. The critics had slammed MacArthur and Hecht's previous work, *Ladies and Gentlemen,* ensuring its financial demise.

Hayes was performing in a play called *Coquette* at the time. But renowned producer Jed Harris, who produced both shows, canceled *Coquette* for that evening so Hayes could attend *The Front Page.*

She sat in the balcony to be near MacArthur and Hecht , both of whom were so nervous they were standing outside on a fire escape awaiting the audience's verdict.

While the first act was still being performed, Hayes heard the laughter and knew in her heart the show was destined for success. She got up from her seat, hurried onto the fire escape, and leaped into MacArthur's arms, babbling enthusiastically.

MacArthur listened to Hayes pour out her adulation as he held her tight. Then he held her at arm's length, looked deeply into her eyes, and asked if Hayes would marry him.

"You took the words right out of my mouth," she beamed.

They were married three days later.

Another great theater marriage was that of actress Kitty Carlisle and playwright Moss Hart. Carlisle, however, stopped performing after the marriage. It was only in 1970, many years after Hart's passing, that Harold Kennedy persuaded her to return to the stage and do four successive summer stock tours with him.

The first three years, she starred in Hart's *Light Up the Sky;* in year four, it was a play Kennedy had written for her, *Don't Frighten the Horses.* During the three years and six hundred performances of

Light Up the Sky, Kennedy and Carlisle had a ritual they observed every night.

At the end of the first act, Carlisle always sent the stage manager to Kennedy's dressing room to relay the same message: "Tell Mr. Kennedy I'm not going on in the second act until he tells me where he is taking me to supper."

There is no play more steeped in mystery, fear, and superstition than Shakespeare's *Macbeth*. Those in the theater often use the synonym "the Scottish play." "That play" and "the Unmentionable" have also sufficed for those who are afraid to say the title aloud. Some also believe a curse can come from quoting lines from the play or using any props, costumes, or sets from previous productions of you-know-what.

This tradition of terror may have its roots in the witches in the play. There is also an undeniably disturbing history of production disasters, beginning with the play's original presentation on August 7, 1606. Young Hal Berridge was playing Lady Macbeth. (It was the custom in Elizabethan theater to have men and boys play all roles.) It is said that Berridge died backstage during that first *Macbeth* and, frankly, things have not gone that well since.

The Guardian theater critic Michael Billington has cited numerous British brouhahas regarding the Scottish play at the Old Vic. In 1934, four different actors were forced to play Macbeth in a single week. Malcolm Keen lost his voice. Alistair Sim came down with a chill. Marius Goring was deemed unacceptable by Old Vic head Lilian Baylis and replaced by John Laurie.

The 1937 production featuring Laurence Olivier was postponed three days after a change of directors and then, the death of Baylis. Olivier narrowly escaped death when a stage weight came crashing down.

During the 1954 Old Vic production, a large painting of Baylis fell off the wall and smashed onto a bar on opening night.

Peter O'Toole would have done well to take these portents to heart, but he starred in a 1980 production at the Old Vic nevertheless. He entered covered from head to toe in stage blood—almost as if he knew what was coming, critically speaking. It was savaged in the reviews. One reviewer called it ". . . not so much downright bad as heroically ludicrous." Another reported, "One has to suppress the urge to guffaw."

Frank Loesser's *Guys and Dolls* was the highlight of his career. But when he wrote the music and lyrics for *Greenwillow*, which ran for little more than two months at the Alvin Theatre, his career was waning.

On closing night, the performers and crew had the opportunity backstage to read the wire sent by Loesser, who was in London at the time.

It simply read, "Oops! Sorry!"

Malcolm Hardee is known as much for his practical jokes offstage as for those he tells onstage. He spent three years in prison for stealing a member of Parliament's Rolls-Royce. Hardee, who once toured a pornographic version of a Punch-and-Judy puppet show for adults, has saved his most outrageous behavior, however, for the Edinburgh Fringe Festival.

Once, while attending a show by a feminist theater collective known as Monstrous Regiment, he stopped the show from the audience, announcing with great regret that he had just read that actress Glenda Jackson had died. He asked, in the spirit of the festival, that one minute of silence be observed in her honor. Monstrous Regiment respectfully agreed.

But after the minute was up, their respect went out the window. Hardee took out a newspaper clipping, studied it, and then declared, "I'm sorry, it's not Glenda Jackson. It's Wendy Jackson, an old-age pensioner."

Hardee's most outrageous interruption of a live act also occurred at Edinburgh, where he and monologuist Eric Bogosian were performing in two tents next to each other. Hardee was irritated by Bogosian's use of loud taped heavy metal music. In a fit of pique that sincerely raises the question of Hardee's sanity, he took a small tractor and drove it, naked no less, through the tent where Bogosian was performing, followed by the forty-four people who'd been watching Hardee perform.

Bogosian was livid. This is not surprising, especially if you have seen the intensity of his performances. He had to be physically restrained in his dressing room from smashing in Hardee's face.

"They drove a fucking tractor through my show!" Bogosian is quoted as screaming, angrily though fairly accurately.

Hardee, it seems, did not know when to quit. A year later, he learned that Bogosian was to tape a show for Channel Four in the Albany Empire. This time borrowing a forklift, Hardee bribed a technician to open the loading-dock door to the studio just as Bogosian was to go onstage. But the forklift was six inches too tall.

Luckily, Hardee and Bogosian live on different continents. Otherwise, their wrath might destroy whole communities.

Before *The Cocoanuts* was the hilarious film by the Marx Brothers, it was onstage at the Lyric Theatre, with music by Irving Berlin and book by George S. Kaufman. Berlin and Kaufman did not get along that well. When the music was on, Kaufman would sidle into the lobby, and when the performers were speaking, Berlin tended to do the same.

Kaufman was not too happy with the amount of lines changed by the Marx Brothers, either. One night, at the back of the house, Kaufman was listening to a story told by writer Heywood Broun. Broun also wrote book reviews and was known as a raconteur and someone who actually brought books into the theater to read in case he was bored with the play. However, Kaufman stopped Broun's story and moved down an aisle toward the front of the stage.

He soon returned, and Broun asked him why he'd interrupted him.

"I had to," Kaufman insisted. "I thought I heard one of the original lines from the show."

Some performers are said to have voices that can move people to tears. While that is so, Phyllis Neilson-Terry had a voice that went one step beyond.

In the 1930s, Neilson-Terry played a variety of Shakespearean roles, frequently in the Open Air Theatre in Regent's Park in

London. She was tall and powerful and her coloratura voice easily reached the back row when she played Oberon in *A Midsummer Night's Dream.*

In fact, it is said that when she delivered the speech that begins, "I know a bank . . ." her voice reached the zoo, hundreds of yards away, awakening wolves and hyenas who would then howl accompaniment to her soliloquy.

The great dancer and choreographer Rudolf Nureyev did a tour of *The King and I* that took him and Liz Robertson, as Anna, to Miami. Near the end of the first act, Nureyev nearly missed his entrance. During the scene in which he is being instructed on how to convince the British that he is not a barbarian, Nureyev was distracted.

At one point, he moved toward the wings and called off to the stage manager, "Matt, the phone." Inasmuch as there were very few phones in nineteenth-century Siam, this puzzled the audience, as did the wild gesticulations Nureyev directed toward the offstage area while Robertson was explaining to him how to be polite.

When the Rodgers and Hammerstein musical ended, Nureyev ran like the wind for his dressing room, not at all interested in curtain calls. He had been interrupted while making a long-distance call to Paris and, when he ran onstage, he had neglected to hang up. The call, which took up a large portion of the second act, was being charged to him.

The playwright Ronald Harwood worked in many capacities with the renowned actor Sir Donald Wolfit. Harwood variously served as student, stage manager, actor, and dresser alongside the eccentric performer.

Offstage, some of Wolfit's actions were as memorable as those onstage. Harwood recalled that Wolfit could harshly criticize a fellow actor for ruining a scene moments before he walked onstage for his own next bit.

The first entrance in a play, for Wolfit, was also remarkable. Harwood recalled that, as he prepared in the wings, a dresser attended him, bearing a silver tray with a glass of Guinness on it, along with a few peeled grapes and a chamois cloth with which to pat his face. The length of the show determined how many Guinnesses would be consumed offstage. And woe to any actor who approached Wolfit while he pondered his roles in the wings. It was not unknown for Wolfit to spit grape seeds at the intruder.

Once, an assistant stage manager by the name of Sally Bussell forgot to put out an important prop during the play *A New Way to Pay Old Debts* by Phillip Massinger. The oversight created a series of problems at the end, ruining Wolfit's final, dramatic exit.

After the curtain calls, Bussell, anticipating Wolfit's rage, ran to him in the wings, fell on her knees crying, and gasped, "I'm so sorry."

The great actor, his rage diminished by this wise display of contrition, held up his right hand with an effortless grandeur and intoned, "I absolve you."

The night in the theater that most haunts actor Greg Kramer was, fittingly, Halloween night, 1984. At Vancouver's TheatreSpace,

Kramer was playing Mephistopheles in part one of Goethe's *Faust*.

In his final scene, Kramer appeared through a trap door in the stage floor in order to drag Faust back down into hell. But things became hellish for Kramer when he looked around for assistance to boost him up into the trap door. The assistant stage manager was off for the night, and the replacement was nowhere to be seen. Kramer, knowing his cue was arriving, desperately ran around in horns and tail and pitchfork, looking for anyone backstage to lift him up through the trap door. Everyone was apparently onstage at the time.

Knowing he'd be eternally damned if he missed his entrance, Kramer ran outside the theater and, in his devil outfit, accosted the first two persons he met, explaining what he needed. In the spirit of Halloween, the two pedestrians agreed.

Kramer speedily gave them instructions on boosting him up through the trap door and when he hissed "Go!" they did as they were told. Kramer made his entrance and breathed an internal sigh of relief. He had brilliantly saved a potential disaster.

But when Mephistopheles casually looked back to the other side of the stage, he saw the head of one of the street volunteers, looking around in amazement.

In February 1932, Sophie Tucker returned from a triumphant tour of Europe to the only theater still presenting vaudeville on Broadway, the Palace Theatre. Movies were taking over, and most people in the theater community felt the Palace was doomed to go the same route.

One Wednesday, when Tucker was onstage singing for all she was worth, she noticed the stage manager in the wings frantically signaling to her. Tucker ignored him and continued with the song.

When she glanced over the next time, there was a crowd, urging Tucker with hand motions to get off the stage. Some began pointing upward. Tucker looked in that direction to see a long flame shooting out of the flies above them.

Tucker was convinced that if she immediately left the stage, panic would ensue in the packed house. She addressed the crowd. "Take it easy, folks. Don't run. Give everybody a chance to get out."

The front and side doors of the theater were opened, but in the process, the draft of air fanned the flames above Tucker. She was dressed in a gown covered with bronze sequins and knew that if so much as a spark should hit her, she would instantly go up in flames. Still, like a captain committed to going down with the ship, Tucker continued singing as the patrons retreated until the property boy yanked her off the stage and the steel fire curtain came down.

The damage was minimal, confined to the flies and part of the orchestra seats.

Tucker's bravery was rewarded by the newspapers the next day.

One headline read: "Red-Hot Mama Burns Up Palace Theatre." Another trumpeted, "Sophie's Songs So Hot, Theatre Burns Under Them!"

Not long after Laurence Olivier's *Hamlet* was described in the press as ". . . the tragedy of a man who could not make up his mind," Orson Welles was in London with his production of *Moby Dick*.

Critic Kenneth Tynan and television writer Ian Dallas were

present on opening night when the false nose Welles was wearing fell off his face and onto the stage.

Dallas leaned over to Tynan and murmured, "The tragedy of a man who could not make up his nose."

The comment found its way into Tynan's review, though its author was not credited.

One of the most notorious theater murders in English history is that of actor William Terris. The well-liked "Breezy Bill," as he was known, was just opening the stage door to London's Adelphi Theatre one night in 1897 when a jealous, recently fired actor, Richard Arthur Prince, stabbed him to death with a kitchen knife. The death stunned the theater community.

In 1928, a man claimed he saw a ghost, a tall man in a gray suit and homburg hat, in Maiden Lane. He later identified the man, via a photograph, as William Terris.

To this day, there are occasional sightings of Terris's ghost at the Covent Garden underground station, which is on the grounds of a bake shop Terris used to visit.

One ticket collector refused to work at the Covent Garden station after swearing that Terris's ghost had appeared, pushed down on his head, and then disappeared.

The night he was murdered, Terris was entering the Adelphi to star in a play called *Secret Service*.

Gwen Verdon, in a television interview, recalled a time when she performed "If My Friends Could See Me Now" and, in fact, hardly anyone could see her.

When *Sweet Charity* was running at the Palace Theatre on Broadway, Verdon always performed that song in a follow spot. One night, the follow spot didn't. It was nowhere to be seen. So Verdon performed the song standing in the same location on the stage.

She was wearing a hat and she used it to cover her face and tell the stage manager in the wings that the lighting was wrong. The stage manager got the message and went up to the lighting booth.

The reason Verdon's friends couldn't see her then was that the lighting operators were found tied up and gagged. It was payday at the theater, and someone had mugged them.

The highly praised actor William Charles Macready was also known to be ever "Macready" with his tongue and his fists.

Once, in Norwich, while playing Hamlet, he had given the actor in the role of Claudius a very harsh criticism offstage. It came back to haunt him, as Claudius decided to die center stage, a spot usually reserved for Macready's death.

The even-more-than-usual Melancholy Dane whispered angrily to his Claudius, "Get up and die elsewhere, sir!"

To this, Claudius sat up and, in a voice very far from a stage whisper, he bellowed, "Mr. Macready, but I'm king now. And I shall die just where I like."

During Macready's performance of Shylock in *The Merchant of Venice*, he was in the wings, preparing to rage onstage, when a fan approached him. Macready rained blows on the man just before making his furious entrance.

Afterward, Macready assumed the stage manager had arranged for the man to accost him in order to fuel Macready's anger for the sake of the performance. It had worked. Macready asked the stage manager how to reach the man to repay him.

"At present, sir," said the uneasy stage manager, "they have conveyed him to the hospital."

Yet, even among these indiscretions, Macready's most atrocious behavior—albeit in service to his craft—took place in Manchester. There Macready, playing Macbeth, would each night have a stagehand dye his hands with cochineal, a red dye made from the bodies of insects, in order to simulate blood.

But, as noted above, one should never expect everything to go right during the Scottish play, and for one performance, the stagehand was nowhere to be seen. Desperate to effect the proper image, Macready went up to a fan hanging about in the wings and punched him in the nose. The actor who knew no bounds then dipped his hands in the innocent man's blood, as if washing up before dinner, and made his entrance.

The victim was paid five pounds for inadvertently sticking his nose into Macready's business.

Peter Hall's first season at Stratford-upon-Avon featured a fine company of hard drinkers, including Peter O'Toole and Jack Mac-Gowran. The latter once arrived utterly sloshed just before a performance, and fellow actor Dinsdale Landen advised Hall of it, convinced MacGowran could barely stand, let alone act.

Hall was already less than enamored of MacGowran. They had exchanged heated words after one rehearsal, which ended with

MacGowran shouting, "Peter Hall, there's a lot of people in the world. But you're not one of them."

Hall told Landen he had a faultless concoction that would make MacGowran both throw up and sober up. He instructed Landen to use his "old RAF cure," which was a cup of water mixed with a lot of salt and tobacco.

They both presented the cure, without describing its ingredients, to MacGowran. He swallowed it down, blinked, grimaced, and then held out the cup.

They asked how he felt, waiting for him to dash madly for the toilet.

"I'm all right," said the two-fisted drinker, "but could I have just one more?"

The great performers make their audiences wonder how they do what they do. But for fellow performers who witness excellence night after night, the question arises: How do the best in the business better themselves?

Laurence Olivier had been performing *Othello* in London, and, one night, he exceeded his usual brilliance. The astounded cast greeted him warmly backstage at the end of the show, applauding him for the transcendent performance.

Olivier, scowling inexplicably, slammed his dressing room door.

One of the company members bravely knocked and said, "What's the matter, Larry? It was great."

"I know it was great," the star miserably agreed, "but I don't know how I did it, so how can I be sure I can do it again?"

Why do patrons wait just before an opening curtain to go to the bathroom? It is a question Todd Shotz asked himself when he was in attendance at Noël Coward's *Waiting in the Wings* at the Walter Kerr.

As most of the audience readied for Lauren Bacall and Rosemary Harris to play two former actresses in a retirement home, a man in the mezzanine decided it was the perfect time to go to the men's room. In the darkness he tripped, and he rolled, ass over teakettle, down the stairs toward the railing of the mezzanine, tumbling past Shotz.

His wife's scream echoed throughout the theater. Luckily, the man did not fall out of the mezzanine onto the floor below, but the incident kept the performers literally waiting in the wings for forty-five minutes.

For many people of an artistic persuasion, the hardest audience to please is neither critic nor fellow artist.

It's your parents.

Anthony Shaffer was at the opening of fellow playwright Harold Pinter's *The Homecoming* when he bumped into Pinter's father.

Rather than expressing pride in his son's work, the elder Pinter told Shaffer to inform Harold that the public did not really like his work. Furthermore, Pinter's father wanted Shaffer to see if Pinter couldn't ". . . brighten it up a bit."

The old adage is "Sex sells." But not on Broadway in 1928.

Moments after the curtain went up on *Pleasure Man,* the New York Police Department raided the theater and the entire cast was dragged off to jail. The play was a detailed observation of life backstage among gay male dancers, female impersonators, a handsome leading man who seduced every woman he could, and other colorful theater professionals.

The *Evening Standard* review bleated, ". . . such filth as turns one's stomach to even remember." The playwright and producer were charged with presenting "an obscene, indecent, immoral and impure drama." Yes, but was it entertaining?

The playwright managed to get the cast released from jail in time to make the next day's matinee. This time, the NYPD showed commendable restraint. They waited until intermission before arresting all fifty-four performers, still in costumes and makeup. It closed after, technically speaking, one half of a performance.

But the playwright, also an actress, went on to conquer not only the stage but the screen. The playwright eventually became known and revered for the very same bawdiness that ruined *Pleasure Man* and earlier productions.

The playwright later achieved the status of being the highest-paid woman in show business.

The playwright was Mae West.

Al Jolson, in many ways, was ambivalent about singing and acting.

He didn't take singing lessons until the age of thirty-five and then quit after the sixth lesson because he claimed the instruction was hurting his voice.

The great showman Billy Rose recalled the night in 1921 when Jolson was in the Broadway musical *Bombo,* with music by Sigmund Romberg and book and lyrics by Harold Atteridge. Halfway through the second act, Jolson abruptly stopped, crossed downstage to the footlights, and asked, humbly, "Do you want the rest of this plot or would you rather have me sing a few songs?"

The audience indicated its preference for the latter, the cast was sent home, and Jolson, taking off his coat and settling in, performed until one o'clock in the morning, at which time he had to beg the people to go home and let him get some rest.

Jolson, however, was subject to terrible bouts of stage fright, despite his iconic standing in show business. One night, he did not arrive before the curtain at the Winter Garden, and, shortly after eight, he was found outside, wandering in the rain, clearly disturbed. He was gently convinced to come inside the theater and later to perform.

Another night, in Chicago, Jolson showed his tolerance for inconvenience . . . and cold weather. Returning to his hotel in the biting Chicago night air, he saw a neon sign that read, "It's June in Miami."

With absolutely no concern for the theater management, Jolson did not bother to tell them before he left the show and headed for the sunshine of Miami.

The actor and playwright Charles Macklin was one of the most respected stage performers of eighteenth-century England, especially for his heavily researched and earnest portrayal of Shylock in *The Merchant of Venice.*

Unfortunately, his reputation is a tiny bit tainted by his having killed a fellow actor . . . because of a wig.

While readying himself to go onstage as a servant in a play at the Royal Theatre Drury Lane in 1735, Macklin searched in frustration for a particular wig he liked. He found it, but—alas, it was on the head of actor Thomas Hallam.

Macklin convinced Hallam to give him the wig, but one assumes there was a great deal of anger, arrogance, and presumption in the discussion. This is not a wild assumption, as Hallam threw the wig at Macklin, who was so infuriated at the reaction that he took the cane he was leaning on and thrust it at Hallam's face.

It went right through one of Hallam's eyes, killing him.

Macklin, rather than going onstage that night, surrendered himself to the authorities. He conducted his own defense and was acquitted, which enabled him to have a respected acting career, author nine plays, and live to the ripe old age of ninety-seven.

Lerner and Loewe's smash musical *My Fair Lady* had a very rough start. Its first tryout in New Haven was scheduled for February 4, 1956, just in time for a huge blizzard.

Rex Harrison felt insecure about the show and, using the snowstorm as a further excuse, insisted he would need another day of rehearsal with the orchestra, and that the show would not go on until the Monday night premiere. With that, he locked himself in his dressing room a mere three hours before curtain.

The house manager at the Shubert Theatre in New Haven was told of this cancellation. A local radio bulletin announced the sudden change in schedule. But many locals had not heard it, and by six o'clock, there was a huge mob outside the theater, shivering in the snow, demanding to be admitted.

The manager anticipated a potential riot, or at least a hostile snowball fight, if the show did not go on as planned. He contacted producer Herman Levin and nastily asserted, "Harrison deserted."

Levin arrived in a big hurry and pounded on Harrison's locked dressing room door, demanding that the finicky star come out and get ready to perform. From inside, Harrison refused.

Finally, desperation drove Levin to tell Harrison that the bad publicity resulting from his petulance would harm his future career.

Mulling this over, Harrison suddenly had a change of heart. He opened the door and told the panic-stricken faces before him that in loyalty to the rest of the company, he would go on.

This was very magnanimous of Harrison, but a problem remained. The cast had been told of Harrison boycotting that night's performance, and so they had dispersed to spend the night as they wished in New Haven.

As the audience was allowed inside, theater personnel were running all over town, trying to find the cast members. They were rounded up from movie theaters, bars, and health clubs. Amazingly, they were all found. The show started late, at 8:40 P.M.

Harrison had no idea how close he came to ruining a major career move. *My Fair Lady* held the record for Broadway performances for years and won Harrison both the Tony and Oscar awards.

5

Hard Shoes to Fill
(Actors' Movements Onstage)

LAURENCE OLIVIER, DESPITE his stature as a great actor and director, was so petrified with stage fright regarding the London opening of *The Merchant of Venice* that he instructed actor Anthony Nicholls and others in the cast to not look directly at his face onstage. They complied, giving him only sidelong glances while performing.

The last time John Gielgud performed *Hamlet* was at the Cairo Opera House. Afterward, he had plenty of reason to be a Melancholy Dane. The man playing Horatio uttered his line, as expected: "My Lord, I think I saw him yesternight," and promptly went into an epileptic fit and fell into Gielgud's arms, writhing uncontrollably.

Gielgud immediately shouted angrily to the prompt corner, "Drop the curtain. Put something in his teeth. Fetch the understudy."

On top of this, it was a school matinee for local children.

John Gielgud's actor friend Esme Percy had helped him direct the London production of *The Lady's Not for Burning*. Percy, who had lost one eye when it was bitten out by a dog, was too vain to wear an eye patch while onstage in the play. Sure enough, his glass eye popped out of his head one night and rolled onto the floorboards, bringing the play to a screeching halt.

Fellow actor Richard Leech, also a director, decided to pick up the eye.

Overcome with concern, Percy said aloud, "Oh, do be careful. Don't tread on it. They cost eight pounds each."

Gielgud convinced Percy to wear an eye patch, albeit grudgingly, for the rest of the run.

Darrell Larson was a performer in a series of interconnected plays by Murray Mednick entitled *The Coyote Cycle*. The seven plays were site-specific, generally performed outdoors, and involved American Indian myths and characters.

Plays 1 through 3 were to receive an all-night performance at the Paramount Ranch, the back lot in Malibu that the film studio used for shooting Western movies. Fellow actor Norbert Weisser would be buried in earth and pop out of it to begin the play, and Larson would leap from a tree and land on his feet, delivering his first lines.

But at the Paramount Ranch, the smallest tree they could find for the first *Coyote* play was an oak, twenty feet tall. Ropes were rigged so that Larson could slide, rather than jump, down to begin his role.

It was a nice try. But Larson, nevertheless, slipped off a rope, plunged to the earth, landed oddly, and shattered one of his heels. Of course, he was performing barefoot.

With pain so acute he felt it from his feet to the top of his skull, Larson delivered his first line and continued the entire night, without telling Weisser, Mednick, or anyone else. Except one person.

The only person to learn of his injury during the all-night performance was a friend who literally carried Larson on his back to the sites for the second and third plays at the Paramount Ranch. By the time they were finished, well after midnight, Larson was in convulsions and was taken to an emergency clinic doctor, who said there was nothing to do but stay off his feet for six weeks.

Two weeks later, Larson returned to finish the run of *The Coyote Cycle.*

George Bernard Shaw's *The Philanderer* opened at the Mermaid Theatre in London with a specially designed parquet floor. It was so special that when actress Jane Arden made her entrance, she sailed across its highly polished surface and landed on a little old lady in the audience.

Arden was very roughed up, and so her understudy went on as the play began again.

The understudy made the same entrance, slipped in the same way, and landed on the exact same little old lady.

During intermission, grit was applied to the stage. But that did not help the little old lady, who had left the theater after the second actress had landed on her, assuming the same thing might keep happening all night long.

Sammy Davis Jr. was known as a triple threat—a singer, dancer, and actor. Although he had lost an eye in a car accident and used a glass eye in its place, his greatest challenge may have been onstage at the London Palladium. He was in *Golden Boy,* the Charles Strouse Lee Adams musical version of the Clifford Odets play. Dance captain Jacqui Daryl should have been demoted to dance private after accidentally punching Davis in what had been, up to that point, his good eye, causing him to be temporarily totally blind.

However, Mr. Show Business, as he was also known, bravely carried on, and that may not have been for the best, as he then ploughed into three dancers and fell headfirst into the audience.

The first night of entertainment in Sir Oswald Stoll's newly refurbished Coliseum in 1904 London was a smash. Not a smash *hit*— just something that went *smash.*

The Derby was a performance featuring pickpockets, fine ladies, crowds, mounted police, and six jockeys on live horses, all moved by a turntable Due to a failure in the braking mechanism, the turntable, which should have turned no faster than fifteen miles per hour, hit a speed that would do a quarter horse proud.

Actors, horses, bits of the set, and properties all went flying out into the audience. Unfortunately named lead jockey Fred Dent flew into the side of a box and expired before reaching Charing Cross Hospital.

Moss Hart's first play, *The Beloved Bandit,* wasn't very beloved. Seventeen producing organizations passed on it before it was finally staged by Augustus Pichou Jr., respectfully referred to in the theater community as "King of the One-Night Stands."

On opening night in Chicago prior to a presumed run in New York, Hart saw so many things go wrong that a lesser man would have killed himself—or at least quit playwriting forever.

The curtain jammed as the lights dimmed for the beginning of the play, and that should have been a loud and clear omen of disaster. Then the set, a hideous shade of green, crumbled and clobbered a character actor.

After a delay to secure the set, Joseph Regan, a stocky actor six feet four inches tall, entered singing a ballad. He reached the hearts of the audience by tripping on a stage brace and falling into a fireplace. He picked himself up, cursing.

The rain had been falling all day in sheets for Hart's infamous opening night, and at that moment it began to hail with such force that the clatter on the roof of the theater drowned out the dialogue onstage for the next twenty minutes.

The set continued to haunt them. Doors either would not open or doorknobs came away in actors' hands. The leading lady, at one point in the disaster, opened a window to call for Regan's character. The window frame came loose and she was stuck holding it, center stage.

Act 2 was no better. Regan again entered and, unbelievably, tripped over the same brace and fell into the same fireplace. This time, the fireplace collapsed under the pressure of his weight. In act 3, the lumbering Irishman took no chances. In order to avoid the stage brace that had twice felled him, Regan actually entered through the fireplace. Realizing he needed some sort of explanation for this unplanned blocking, he came up with a non sequitur: "Every day's Christmas when the Irish come to town."

When the final curtain fell, there wasn't even a whisper of applause to be heard. The actors took their bows to a sea of rapidly retreating backs. Hart wrote later that the exodus from the theater suggested that twenty-dollar gold pieces were being distributed free in the street outside.

London's The Little Theatre was destroyed in 1941 by a German bomb, but before that sad event, it suffered another bomb: the production of *The Saloon*. The play has a moment when a ghost appears, eerily lit by a red light held by an actress walking across the stage in otherwise complete darkness.

One night the actress lost her way, walked too close to the edge of the stage, and fell into the lap of a man in the audience. She'd knocked herself unconscious. The actors, not knowing what had happened to her, went on with the play. After it was over and all the patrons had left, she was discovered, still unconscious but politely propped up in a sitting position in the front row.

Noël Coward probably wished he'd stuck with writing and composing when he performed in *The Constant Nymph* in London in 1926.

At play's end, the character of Tessa, played by Edna Best, dies of a heart attack. Lewis Dodd (Coward) lifts her body onto the bed, dramatically thrusts open the window, and announces, "Tessa's got away; she's safe; she's dead." Then Dodd bursts into tears and the curtain falls on this powerful tragedy.

But the third night of the play, the sash cord broke on the window, prompting it to come down painfully on Coward's hands.

His line became, "Tessa's gone away; she's safe; she's OW!"

The dead Tessa sat bolt upright to see what had happened, and the curtain fell, to peals of laughter.

Carl Reiner was the master of ceremonies at the Young Musicians Foundation dinner at the Beverly Hilton Hotel in Beverly Hills. No fewer than 1,100 people in formal dress had shown up for the benefit, featuring an orchestra of performers, none older than twenty years of age.

Reiner had been briskly walking on- and offstage during the festivities. When he made a rapid reappearance to present Henry Mancini with a baton to conduct the orchestra, he suddenly felt a searing pain in his right leg and collapsed onstage.

"I think something bad just happened," he said, drawing laughter from the crowd. But Reiner was not kidding around. He was literally unable to stand and take a bow after the seeming pratfall. He was forced to utter, atypically, a cliché: "Is there a doctor in the house?"

While Reiner was attended to, still lying on the stage at the Beverly Hilton, comedian Louis Nye was pulled out of the audience and suddenly became the new MC.

The paramedic arrived and insisted on slitting open Reiner's pant leg with scissors to examine his injury, which later was revealed to be a snapped tendon in his right patella (kneecap).

Never one to lie down on the job, as the paramedic pulled out the scissors, Reiner shouted, in mock horror, "No! Not my lucky tuxedo pants!"

He was carried away to great applause.

Charles Laughton played Galileo for Bertolt Brecht during the Los Angeles production. But the portly and temperamental actor posed a couple of challenges.

First, he would fall into what were considered psychosomatic slumbers, states of sleep so deep, he could only be awakened with much shaking and shouting.

Also, Laughton found some stage business that Brecht's wife, Helene Weigel, found very distasteful. He would, during early scenes in *Galileo*, put his hands in his pockets and fumble about with his genitals.

Weigel was so annoyed at this habit that she sewed up the pockets to Laughton's pants so that he could no longer "play pocket pool."

Laughton was enraged when he could no longer play with himself onstage and insisted, successfully, that his pants pockets be restored.

The great Shakespearean actor Edmund Kean said, "Dying is easy. Comedy is hard." Buster Keaton might have amended that statement to read, "Film is easy. Live slapstick is hard."

Before his film career, Keaton performed with his family on the vaudeville circuit and only missed one performance.

When he was eight years old, Keaton was doing a sketch with his father at Poli's Theatre in New Haven. In the bit, Buster uses a doorway and his physical prowess to pretend he is being attacked. His father, playing his father, immediately comes to his aid to attack the nonexistent assailant. Keaton the Elder then does battle with the unseen half of Buster, including some outlandish kicks.

Unfortunately, one of those kicks went right to Buster's head, literally. He fell to the stage unconscious, and his stunned father lifted him up and carried him out of the theater and across the street to their hotel room.

For eighteen hours, Buster could not be roused. When he was semicoherent, doctors told him he was lucky the kick had struck the back of his head rather than his skull, which might have permanently disabled or killed him.

Buster asked what time it was, and when his mother told him it was just before the afternoon matinee at Poli's, he popped up and insisted on performing.

Mister Keaton, pacing the stage, was stunned to see his son.

"I just won't take any falls today, Pop," Buster assured him. When his father continued to express worry about him going on with the show, Buster smiled. "I'll be all right, if you just make sure you don't kick me in the head again."

When Stephen Sondheim wrote the musical *Gypsy*, his memorable number was "Let Me Entertain You." While the 1995 Valley Performing Arts production of *Gypsy* in a small Alaskan town was entertaining in its way, it was doubtless not what Sondheim had in mind.

First of all, right from the top, during the initial performance of "Let Me Entertain You," the young actress playing Baby Rose threw up repeatedly.

Clearly a trouper, she continued to perform, as did the rest of the cast, ad-libbing and sidestepping vomit as best they could.

After the number was over, a stagehand raced on with a mop and proceeded to smear the contents of Baby Rose's stomach over a wider area.

Following this explosive opening number, another stagehand had to stand behind a wall, holding a plaque—essential to the plot—that refused to stay on the wall. His white knuckles were clearly visible for the whole scene.

It seemed for a short while that the production was going to improve. But that was before people began falling and noisily dropping things backstage.

After one particularly loud backstage crash, a small dog belonging to the character of Mama Rose was heard to squeal in pain.

It did not reappear on stage for the rest of the night.

Dick Shawn was such a hilarious, unpredictable, unique, and innovative performer that when he actually died of a heart attack onstage, everyone laughed, thinking it was part of his act.

Admittedly, Shawn was known for his brilliant one-man show, *The Second Greatest Entertainer in the World,* during which he lay inert onstage, covered in newspaper, for the entire intermission.

On April 17, 1987, Shawn was performing at the University of California, San Diego. He was doing a bit about nuclear war, about the devastation that would be wrought by it. No one would survive, he claimed, except the audience in the small, sheltered theater.

"And I would be your leader!" he shouted and then fell forward, flat on his face.

The audience laughed and waited. They continued to wait, and chuckle, wondering what he would do next. Shawn's son Adam was in the audience, and he suspected something was wrong.

Dick Shawn had died on the spot of a heart attack.

New York Post columnist Cindy Adams later reminded her readers of what Shawn had said about finding the right audience for his challenging, daring comedy: "I can't work places like Vegas or the Catskills, where people are belching. Maybe I belong in colleges. At least if I die, I die in front of intelligent people who know what I'm talking about."

It was Laurie O'Brien's job, as the title character in *Mary Barnes*, playing at the Odyssey Theatre in West Los Angeles, to thrash about and scream on occasion. She was, after all, playing a historical character, a mentally ill woman treated by the noted psychologist R. D. Laing, in this David Edgar drama.

When O'Brien dropped a wine bottle onstage during the play, it shattered. When she had to hysterically fall to the floor later on, bits of glass cut her.

Once she was offstage for a brief transition, crew members noted the blood coming out of her in numerous places. O'Brien refused to halt the production. So, the stage was cleaned up, the bleeding was staunched, makeup was applied to the cuts, and off O'Brien went, to continue playing a madwoman.

During intermission, lighting designer Kathi O'Donohue pulled some shards of glass out of O'Brien's skin, but the plucky performer refused to call it quits.

Weeks later, a piece of glass worked its way out of her outer thigh.

Macbeth is a tragedy. But what is really tragic is when a production of it turns it into a comedy.

Richard Nathan was Lennox in a production of the Scottish play at the University of Southern California. He and fellow actors were directed in one scene to enter through the house, walk down an aisle onto the stage, and begin their scene. One night, the lights that illuminated their path were not working.

Nathan, who along with the others had trouble finding his way to the stage in utter darkness, noticed that Alan Hubbs, playing Ross, seemed to be shaking one leg vigorously, as if a small, vicious dog had sunk its teeth into his foot. Finally, as they reached the stage, Nathan noticed Hubbs reach down and remove a woman's purse from his foot. As he was walking down the aisle, one foot had plunged through the straps and he had dragged it all the way to the edge of the stage.

Nathan did his best not to laugh as the actors assembled onstage.

The lights came up . . . on the opposite side of the stage, where no one was standing.

The audience laughed without knowing about the even funnier moment.

Author Al Marill clearly recalls the night he saw the Boston tryout for the musical *Funny Girl*. It was during this pre-Broadway run that Barbra Streisand accidentally made the show a little funnier than it was supposed to be.

At one point, Sydney Chaplin, as Nick Arnstein, was center stage, lying on a chaise longue, singing, while Streisand, as Fanny Brice, prowled around him. Then she sang her part of the duet and, per the direction, leaped onto him.

Except Streisand did not leap *onto* Chaplin so much as leap *over* him, crashing into the wall behind him.

She got up, brushed herself off ceremoniously, resumed her pre-leap position, signaled for the conductor to give her the last couple of bars of music, and landed on target, refusing to let the first disaster rain on her parade.

Marill witnessed a considerably less brave performance during *Grind*, a musical about the world of burlesque, with book by Fay Kanin, music by Larry Grossman and lyrics by Ellen Fitzhugh.

One night during its Broadway run at the Mark Hellinger, it turned into something other than the same old grind.

Marill recalls the footlights exploding and smoke beginning to pour out of them.

They were not wisps of smoke. They were billows of smoke, and members of the audience began to get very nervous. People began to get up and leave the theater, although the show hadn't stopped.

Seeing more and more audience members fleeing up the aisles,

Ben Vereen, in the lead as the character Leroy, panicked. Rather than trying to calm the audience and assure them they would not choke to death from smoke inhalation, he left the stage mid-number.

And he was promptly forced back onstage by the stage manager, who instructed Vereen to assure those remaining that the situation was not serious and that *Grind* would not grind to a halt.

Leos Janácek's opera *The Makropulos Case,* in its first performance at New York's Metropolitan Opera, January 5, 1996, will never be forgotten by those who saw it.

The tenor died onstage. In keeping with the requirements of opera, he did it in an extremely theatrical and colorful fashion.

Richard Versalle, who was sixty-three, played Vitek, a Prague legal clerk, alongside the renowned Jessye Norman. He climbed a ten-foot ladder onstage to file a legal brief, sang the insanely ironic line, "Too bad you can only live so long," had a heart attack, fell from the ladder, and plunged to the stage, dead.

Janácek's opera is about the secret of eternal life.

Jean-Baptiste Poquelin was both one of the theater's greatest dramatists and an actor-manager. In 1673, during the fourth performance of his latest comedy at Paris's Palais Royal, Poquelin, battling consumption, uttered the final line of his play, convulsed, and tried to cover it with a laugh. The curtain came down. Having made it through the entire performance, terribly sick, he then collapsed.

Immediately conveyed to his home in the rue de Richelieu, the playwright-actor was overcome with a fit of coughing, and blood oozed from his mouth. Two clerics were summoned to perform last rites for the fifty-one-year-old artist. When they arrived and learned the identity of the unfortunate man, they refused. A previous comedic play of his had made him, in the eyes of the Church, unworthy of that final blessing.

Another priest was summoned and agreed to come, but he arrived to see the playwright die in the arms of two nuns, friends who had just happened to visit when he was refused a final blessing by the two judgmental priests.

And so it was that Molière, a towering figure in the history of theater, passed away.

His final play, about a hypochondriac who denigrates doctors and yet fears death constantly, was known as *Le Malade Imaginaire,* literally "the hypochondriac," referred to by English-speaking audiences as *The Imaginary Invalid.*

When Budd Schulberg's *On the Waterfront* was staged at the Brooks Atkinson on Broadway in 1995, everyone had great expectations for its success. It boasted a cast including Kevin Conway, Ron Eldard, and James Gandolfini, and of course, had the name recognition provided by the classic film starring Marlon Brando.

Theater critic Judd Hollander was present at a preview when, three lines before the end of act 1, there was a cacophonous, angry mob scene. Actor Jerry Grayson slumped to the ground. The audience assumed it was part of the action.

But Eldard, in the role of Terry Malloy, suddenly dropped his

Brooklyn accent and called desperately for a doctor. Grayson was in the throes of a heart attack and could not breathe.

Within moments, three doctors appeared on the stage, as the audience and performers looked on. Because of where Grayson had fallen, downstage, stagehands were not able to hide him by lowering the curtain.

Thus, those in attendance were subjected to the sight of a doctor pounding on Grayson's chest. When this seemed to fail, another doctor actually took out a scalpel he had on him and prepared to perform an emergency tracheotomy on the stage.

Thankfully, it was not necessary. Grayson was revived and taken to a hospital, and eventually he fully recovered.

At the Brooks Atkinson, the shaken cast had a meeting and decided to continue the play, after a delay of thirty minutes.

It was apparently a bad omen. *On the Waterfront* closed after just eight performances.

Jeanne Haggard directed a production of *Arsenic and Old Lace* at A.C.T. (Area Community Theater) Ottawa! in Kansas. Never has a director's last name so perfectly summed up her feelings after a show.

In her defense, Haggard was saddled with amateur actors, including high school and middle school students, due to the size of the cast required by Joseph Kesselring's play.

On opening night, Nancy Thacker, playing Abby Brewster, got things rolling by completely forgetting all her lines in the opening scene, making it necessary for the other actors to ad-lib their way to coherence until she remembered her role again—although, sadly, she went all the way back to the beginning of the play.

When Haggard went onstage at intermission to help change the set, she noticed lines taped to a pole. Tim Mollett, as Jonathan Brewster, had a scene in which he had to recite all the cities he had visited and all the people he had dispatched. He had secretly consulted with the lines on the pole. She decided to leave it up since the audience could not see it.

But during intermission, Katherine Ochampaugh, cast in the normally male role of Dr. Einstein, had an asthma attack. Someone called 911, an ambulance came, and paramedics carried Ochampaugh away, somewhat prolonging the intermission.

An actor who had not auditioned for the play and was unfamiliar with it was pressed into service to play the role of Dr. Einstein.

Act 2 began with a bang, as Stacy Corbin, playing Martha Brewster, made a grand entrance by falling down an entire flight of stairs.

During a later scene, in candlelight, the new Dr. Einstein had a bit of trouble reading the script she held and figuring out where to move.

But other than that, opening night was an utter success.

Nicola Elson was playing *Two Gentlemen of Verona* and *A Midsummer Night's Dream* in rep in country homes and castles around England in the summer of 2003. In Wadebridge, near Cornwall, she was asked to play an Outlaw in *Two Gentleman.*

The part was not a complex one. It required her to climb a scaffolding wearing a poncho, cowboy hat, and mask and look for the enemy. Upon their entrance, her one line was, "If there be ten of them, shrink not, but down with them."

Elson unconsciously decided Shakespeare did not know how to

get rid of these actors. The words that came out of her mouth were, "If there be ten of them . . . we'll shrink them!"

Very upset that she had suggested reducing the size of actors in Elizabethan England, Elson quickly clambered down from the scaffolding and ran across the stage to hide, per the director, in some foliage.

As she ran, she saw an electrical cord, attached to a keyboard, in her path. She attempted to leap over it on her way to the bushes but miscalculated. One foot hit the cord, and she flew offstage.

She hid her laughter behind a tree as one of the actors picked up the fallen keyboard. He began his final speech, which was to be movingly accompanied by a flutelike keyboard sound. Unfortunately, when Elson knocked over the keyboard, she changed the last preset of a flute tone to that of a bugle horn.

And so, the actor's last soliloquy sounded like it was being delivered at a fox hunt.

The rest of the company insisted that Elson take a special bow at the end for all the damage she had wrought.

The Waldorf-Astoria is famous as a great hotel. The Waldo Astoria, a dinner theater in Kansas City, Missouri, is not so well known. However, the Waldo Astoria has a claim to fame: it is the only theater where props and furniture were auctioned off . . . during a production.

It was toward the end of an eight-week run of Ron Clark and Sam Bobrick's *Murder at the Howard Johnson's* when Dennis Allen, a local comedic actor, turned an accident into an inspired bit of lunacy.

Audiences had been rather lethargic toward the end of the run, and energy onstage had been generally low. Allen found he was not getting the laughs he had when the play opened. One night, at the end of the first act, when he customarily opened a door and exited, a doorknob came off in his hand.

He stood there for a moment, pondering the doorknob, the dull audience, his career. Then Allen turned toward the audience, breaking character, and asked if anyone wanted to buy the doorknob cheap.

Someone in the house called back that he would pay a quarter.

Suddenly Allen came alive, auctioning off the doorknob to those in attendance, as well as getting final bids on a couch, chairs, tables, lamps, and props. As soon as each item had a buyer, Allen would carry it directly to the winning bidder in his seat and collect the money.

The audience, finally waking up, reacted with gales of laughter.

When the stage was bare, Allen told the audience the second act would be coming up and walked off. He went backstage and handed the wad of money to the stage manager—who was not very pleased, for, during intermission, his job was to go back into the house and buy back all the props and furniture and return them to their correct positions onstage.

The noted thespian Edmund Kean shuffled off this mortal coil in a manner befitting a great actor. He died performing Shakespeare alongside his actor son Charles.

Kean was to play another night of *Othello* to his son's Iago at Covent Garden in London on May 15, 1833. His financial situation was as ruinous as his health, so the father did not dare skip the performance.

Upon arriving at the theater, Kean sent for his son, who found him in his dressing room, on the verge of collapse.

"I am very ill, Charlie," Kean intoned. "I am afraid I shall be unable to act."

But with the aid of stimulants and the imploring of his manager, Kean dressed and, leaning on his son, made his way down to the wings.

Covent Garden was jammed that evening, and the much-loved Kean was greeted with thunderous applause. But he was very faint of voice, his movements were labored, and before the performance had run its course, he fell into his son's arms and expired shortly thereafter.

His last words upon the stage were, "Othello's occupation's gone."

Raven Bast is a comedian who continued to perform even after learning she had brain cancer. This would be remarkable enough, but one evening, Bast's life became even more challenging and bizarre.

Despite the fact that she occasionally experienced seizures, she continued doing gigs. And sure enough, at the Sportsmen's Lodge in Studio City, California, in the middle of a comedy routine, she felt a seizure triggered by the stage lights coming on. Realizing that a serious seizure could also prompt a heart attack, Bast immediately stopped performing and announced into the microphone, "Please excuse me. I think I need someone to call 911."

Bast quickly made her way to the ladies' restroom and, for the next ten minutes, lay on the floor of one of the stalls, trying to regain her bearings.

Her solitude was interrupted by the sound of a female audience member who recognized the legs sticking out from under the stall door.

But rather than coming to her rescue, the oblivious woman said, cheerfully, "Oh, honey, that's funny how you make up jokes about supposedly having cancer." Then, realizing that Bast was lying on the bathroom floor, the woman said, "It's probably just gas from your period."

And assuming Bast's problem was menstruation, not brain cancer, she not-so-helpfully tossed a tampon under the stall door and left.

Bast literally crawled out of the bathroom and cried out for an ambulance. She noticed that the booker of the comedy acts had not called for help, or even taken a break between acts.

It affirms the old adage that stand-up comedy is the toughest gig of all. But if you love it, you will do it under any circumstances.

John Gallogly, as a young actor, had a role in the Broadway musical *The Utter Glory of Morrissey Hall* by Clark Gesner, with book co-written by director Nagle Jackson. However, the show was doomed to a bad fate, one that included Gallogly twirling around on a wire above the stage during a love duet and nearly throwing up on one of the great ladies of the theater.

Gallogly played Charles, a young man in love with Helen (Becky McSpadden). He has himself shipped to her in a trunk. But before he arrives, he sends her a letter and the key to the trunk. A love duet is sung while Charles is flown in to the scene, twenty-five feet above the stage.

Unfortunately, this show followed a matinee and a meal of Greek *moussaka* that Gallogly had eaten on Eighth Avenue. Despite the rumbling in his gut, he was not about to ask the one understudy for the male actors, in his mid-forties, to take over on opening night.

So there hung Gallogly, twenty-five feet in the air, hidden in the flies of the Mark Hellinger Theatre, as the scene played out between McSpadden and the great film and stage star Celeste Holm, who had recently turned sixty. Holm was supposed to try to wrestle the key away from McSpadden.

Meanwhile, the stagehand responsible for flying Gallogly jerked the wire and he began to swirl around dizzyingly. The lack of fresh air that high above the stage, coupled with the intense heat of the lights and the memory of the *moussaka,* made Gallogly nauseous. He feared not only ruining the opening night of the musical but vomiting on the head of an acting legend.

Gallogly put his head against a lighting pipe to steady himself, using every ounce of his will to not barf on Celeste Holm, who was violently trying to get the key from McSpadden.

Finally, the scene ended and Gallogly's entrance music began. He was lowered in a rush to about ten feet above the stage, and he and McSpadden began their touching song of love.

But when Gallogly took his head away from the lighting fixture, he released the tension of the wire built up while he was turning around in circles.

As a result, the nauseous Gallogly now began twirling clockwise, then unwinding and twirling counterclockwise, as they sang. McSpadden, stunned, dashed back and forth, trying to make eye contact with him, to show how much she cared. The audience roared with laughter.

John Gallogly can be proud that he did not puke on anyone's head that night. But the show closed after that opening night and in the famous Joe Allen restaurant in Manhattan, there is a drawing depicting this "turkey" of a production.

Still, it was not a complete disaster. Gallogly met a lovely woman named Mary Garripoli because of that haunted production. As of this writing, they have been happily married for twenty-five years.

The site-specific play *Tamara* by John Krizanc is a most unique environmental theater play. It began in Toronto and then ran in other cities, including ten years in Los Angeles, where Karen Kondazian played a lesbian French housekeeper.

The play is really ten plays, with ten characters, set in a mansion, and the audience decides which individual characters to follow through the set. At the end, theatergoers see all the characters together and trade information with other audience members as to what they saw in different rooms, different scenes. The play is set among the decadent upper class of Italy in 1927, as fascism begins to rise.

The play requires split-second timing, so that at the end of one scene, the actors can swiftly move off, followed by a retinue of interested audience members, to the next area and next scene. One night, that clockwork precision was threatened when Kondazian found the shawl she was wearing was caught in the zipper of a patron standing close to her.

Unable to dislodge it, she blithely told the man, "I guess you're going to have to follow me for the rest of the show—or unzip yourself."

The man extricated the shawl from his zipper, whereupon Tony Amendola, playing poet-military man-lover Gabriele d'Annunzio, in keeping with the general decadence of the evening took one of Kondazian's hands, placed it on his crotch, and declared, "I'm next."

It certainly isn't unheard-of for a performer to fall off a stage, especially during a difficult dance number. But what made Sean McDermott's fall at London's Prince of Wales Theatre in Andrew Lloyd Webber's *Starlight Express* so noteworthy were the perfect lyrics he sang just before his demise.

Conductor Paul Bogaev advised McDermott that he had previously been singing too quickly and needed to follow Bogaev on the TV monitors. (There was no orchestra pit.)

McDermott had enough of a challenge roller-skating in the dark, which many have likened to the sensation of floating.

But McDermott did some real floating as he sang the lyrics, "And if you're there, and if you know / Then show me which way I should goooooo—"

He landed in the audience, but immediately popped back up onstage where a pin spot found him.

According to those who saw it, it looked like McDermott had disappeared momentarily into a trap door.

Anyone can fall off a stage and appear foolish or ungainly, garnering cruel chortles in the process. But to fall off a stage on Broadway in such a dramatic way that the audience thinks you are either seriously injured or dead—and then reappear in time for your next cue, is a real art form.

It is something Gina Ferrall, who played Madame Thenardier in *Les Misérables*, can boast of in her resume. In one scene, she ogles money received by her husband for selling poor Cosette. Ferrall would nightly call out, "Ah, you big son of a bitch" and then jump on Thenardier, kissing and hugging him. This ended the scene and always got a big laugh.

However, in what has to be one of the most spectacularly visual accidental pratfalls in Broadway history, one night Ferrall flew past Thenardier and landed on a table. One of the legs of the table broke with a resounding crack, sending her sliding off, headfirst, into the orchestra pit.

Now, the pit had black netting over it because silverware and other small objects often flew off the stage during Trevor Nunn's muscular staging. But the netting was not designed to catch Ferrall, who plummeted through it and disappeared from sight. Some audience members, unsure whether this was part of the show, stood up momentarily and, seeing nothing, returned to their seats.

They could not see Ferrall because she had landed directly on the drums in the pit. The drummer for the show had no cues at that time and was casually reading a magazine when Ferrall plowed into his drum kit.

"Did I just fall into the pit?" she asked, obviously stunned and therefore entitled to an obvious question.

The conductor looked shocked. Onstage, the actress playing Cosette was in tears. This was not because of the character's miserable living conditions. It was because the actress believed Ferrall might be dead.

In fact, the musicians helped Ferrall to her feet. She reentered the backstage area, where cast and crew were stunned to see her not only on her feet and uninjured but running at full speed, shouting, "Get out of my way! I have an entrance!"

Nancy Opel was ready. She was understudying Patti LuPone in the smash hit *Evita* by Lloyd Webber and Rice at the Broadway and she was scheduled to perform.

But before her big moment, things had been so rushed that she had never had a rehearsal on the full set. And no one bothered to tell Opel about the giant cable bundle upstage, behind the balcony representing Casa Rosada, where she entered.

And it was a grand entrance, although not, perhaps, what Opel had hoped for. Wearing an enormous white dress, Opel, as Eva Perón, found herself lying face-first on the stage, in a spotlight, after tripping over the cable.

Mandy Patinkin, as Che Guevara, was unable to help. He was busy singing the now cruelly ironic "High Flying Adored."

Opel wanted to get up on her feet as quickly as possible, but her heels had hooked into her skirt. She described her efforts to get upright in the following manner: "I rocked back and forth like a turtle upside down on its shell."

An actress playing the maid ran to Opel's aid and helped her stand up.

Opel, weaving a bit, decided at the very least to try and account for her fall. Holding her stomach, she announced, "Oh, that uterine cancer is kicking in again."

Dame Edith Evans has a great reputation in the history of English stage. No one, however, will argue that her work in *Crime and Punishment* in 1946 contributed a thing to that reputation.

The adaptation by Rodney Ackland featured Evans playing across from John Gielgud. Evans seemed to have a regular coughing spell each night when Gielgud had a major speech, and Maria Britneva, who played the role of Lady St. Just, grew annoyed.

One evening, Britneva's irritation knew no bounds. Inventing a cure for the common cough, she took a pillow from a sofa, strode over to Evans, and shoved it in her face.

While Western medicine has never recommended this approach, it did seem to have a permanent effect on Evans's cough during *Crime and Punishment.*

When Cindy Lu was nineteen, she was cast in a stage adaptation of Roald Dahl's children's book, *Willy Wonka and the Chocolate Factory,* as a character named Mimi Nintendo. Her first challenge was a day of blocking with a ten-year-old actor in the role of a creature known as an Oompaloompa.

But the real test of Lu's endurance came when she showed up for her performance at Seattle's Pioneer Square Theater with an upset stomach. She would learn later she had a stomach ulcer. As a result, she had not eaten all day and was already lightheaded when she arrived at the theater.

In a scene taking place on a boat going down a river of chocolate, Lu began to get nauseous from the smell of chocolate. She was not imagining it. The director had decided to create an air of realism by strategically placing pans of melting chocolate in the house.

The movements onstage and the chocolate scent, coupled with her stomach ulcer and lack of food, finally got the best of Lu. She turned in the boat to a fellow actor, playing the father of bratty child Veruca Salt, and told him in quiet desperation that she was going to faint and he needed to get her offstage.

On top of it all, the director was using a strobe light as the boat supposedly made its way through the factory. That did it. Lu passed out, and a compassionate xylophone player ran onstage to help revive her and pull her out of the boat.

Her jacket was taken off upstage while the production continued. Lu was asked if she could continue, and she insisted she was all right.

She quickly rejoined the adult actors playing the children. The next scene had them cautiously walking on the edge of a mountain. All the actors carefully pantomimed the process of edging carefully along the dangerous cliff.

All except Lu, who shattered the effect by fainting again.

Even the best improvisational performers, like those at the legendary Second City troupe in Chicago, can do a sketch that goes nowhere. That is why cast member Richard Libertini, fed up with lighting operators terminating bad sketches with blackouts, invented a concept to fix, rather than end, a lousy scene.

Whenever a bit got no laughs or seemed to be going nowhere, Libertini would often enter as "The Improv Police." He would arrest one of the performers, usually the one guiltiest of ruining the sketch, in the name of some offense, and drag that person offstage. Sometimes, Libertini not only arrested a troupe member but inserted himself in the scene as said Improv Policeman, just to see where it would go.

"It wouldn't be as overt as an announcement you were killing the scene," Libertini once explained. "It would be a mysterious arrest."

Patrick Tovatt was playing in Eugene O'Neill's *A Long Day's Journey into Night* at the American Conservatory Theater in San Francisco with his good friend David Grimm. Considering what happened to Tovatt, it is amazing that they stayed friends.

The play required a fight between their characters. At one performance, a blow from Grimm shattered Tovatt's left eardrum.

The play was blocked again, so that lines delivered toward Tovatt's character would reach his right ear, not his left. This worked for the rest of the run. A year later, the play was revived and, at the end of the tour, Grimm, during their fight sequence, put a little bit too much into it and shattered Tovatt's other eardrum.

David Garrick had a thirty-year career as one of the first great actors of the English stage. Yet even he was not immune from embarrassing moments upon the boards. In essaying King Lear, Garrick mesmerized audiences with his performance. But near the end of the play, one very warm May evening, the audience saw Garrick as Lear, bending over Cordelia, suddenly "corpsing," laughing uncontrollably—and then fleeing the stage. Cordelia and Kent did the same.

In the front row, an overweight butcher had brought his mastiff to the performance. As the heat inside the theater grew, the man took off his wig and rested it on the head of the dog.

When Garrick and his fellow players saw the newly groomed dog, they, in the lexicon of American beatniks of the 1950s, "wigged out."

There are three things that can make a fall onstage look ridiculously bad.

One, the outfit you are wearing.

Two, what you say immediately after you fall.

Three, whether you can get up or not.

When Jack Medley was playing the Red Queen in *Through the Looking-Glass* at the Manitoba Theatre Centre in Canada, he managed to score in all three areas.

It was Medley's job to sweep onstage through black mylar and lace as the Red Queen. The outfit was dazzlingly royal. His crown was at least twelve inches tall, he carried an enormous scepter, and his circular velvet train trailed behind him for eight feet.

He was laced into a corset that ran from his neck to his hips, which prevented him from sitting at all. It took the greatest effort simply to look down.

And that was as good a reason as any that, on opening night, Medley wheeled onto the stage and promptly tripped over a knee-high cable that had not been secured. He flew into the air and landed on his face. His landing knocked the breath out of him and he gasped for air. The crown went skittering one way and the scepter the other.

When he regained the ability to speak, he had not yet regained the ability to think.

The first words out of his mouth were, "What the fuck!"

It was, of course, a children's theater production.

And fulfilling the third obligation for disastrous stage falls, Medley could not rise. It was not because he was injured. It was because he was on his back, in a corset, flailing about like an armadillo stuck in quicksand.

About a dozen stagehands dashed over to raise the Red Queen to his/her feet. The curtain came down and they started the play again.

Shakespeare's work has been staged many different ways, and purists sometimes object to certain interpretations. Things can be even more puzzling if not all the actors are following the same guidelines.

In 1938, Ralph Richardson was playing Othello to Laurence Olivier's Iago in a production directed by Tyrone Guthrie. Privately, Olivier convinced Guthrie of the Freudian idea that Iago was secretly in love with Othello.

Guthrie was swayed by Olivier's argument, but did not think that Richardson would find it acceptable. Olivier and Guthrie agreed the actor would give a kiss on the mouth to Richardson's Moor, just on opening night, during a moment of high tension.

After the curtain had fallen, Richardson took Guthrie aside and asked him, with some discomfort, "Tony, have you noticed anything odd about Laurence lately?"

Araby Lockhart performed in a play about Amish country life called *Papa Is All*. But during one performance at the Straw Hat Players,

Canada's first professional summer theater company, Papa took a backseat to Lockhart's unintended actions.

A major scene is structured around a quilting frame, a 12- by 12-foot piece of wood where actors sew and reveal important information that increases the tension in the plot. Lockhart was annoyed as she stitched away, because she could sense restlessness in the audience, even though this was one of the most dramatic moments of the show. Then she and others began to hear titters from a nervous crowd.

Lockhart got up at the appropriate time to make her exit, and that is when she learned what the patrons were sniggering about.

Lockhart had actually sewn her costume to the quilting frame, and could not walk away. She wasn't about to try and drag off the quilting frame, because there was no way it would fit through a 3-by 6-foot door frame. And it was unlikely an Amish woman would strip off her clothes in front of a roomful of people.

So Lockhart, who clearly had put so much of herself into her onstage sewing, suffered the laughter of the house as she ripped her costume away, stitch by agonizing stitch, from the quilt.

As a young actor with the Royal Shakespeare Company, Richard Burton, according to a story he told Robert Goulet, played Prince Hal in *Henry the Fourth, Part 1* at Stratford-upon-Avon. As it was not far from Wales, Burton's brothers came to see him, and they spent the day drinking in pubs. Burton arrived at the theater just in time to get into makeup and put on tights, chain mail, armor, and cape, strap on his broadsword, and step onstage.

He had to urinate, but he figured the adrenaline of performing would soon eliminate the feeling, as it had in the past. Burton was the last actor to exit in act 1 and the first one on in act 2. There was a ten-minute intermission, and not enough time to disrobe, pee, and get dressed again, so he smoked furiously in the wings and tried to ignore his bladder, which was approaching the size of a basketball.

Ten minutes into the second act, Burton was to begin a sword-fight with Michael Redgrave, playing Hotspur. As Burton turned, the day's consumption of alcohol shot out of him like lava pouring down a volcano. Burton, knowing his brothers were among those watching, exerted great effort to stanch the flow of liquid leaking out of his tights.

He drew his broadsword, lunged at Redgrave, and struck at his sword with such force, his own weapon broke off at the hilt. In desperation to win the battle, and now bereft of a weapon, Burton lifted Redgrave with his shoulder and hurled him through some scenery. Burton claimed Redgrave called out, just before his trajectory through the air, "Mind my balls."

Backstage, after Burton was relieved to have relieved himself, Redgrave approached.

"I did think you were perspiring heavily rather heavily, dear boy," Redgrave admitted. "You left large, wet footprints on the stage."

It has been said that great actors can make an audience stop coughing. This is not always so.

Paul Soles had the pleasure of touring with Glenda Jackson and Christopher Plummer in *Macbeth*, a production that eventually found a home on Broadway.

However, it had to pass through Baltimore, where the Scottish play was performed in a concrete theater center built in the 1960s. A phenomenal number of theatergoers were coughing during the performance, and the concrete walls amplified and echoed the sounds.

Soles felt the distraction of the noises, but Plummer and Jackson never let it break their concentration or alter their redoubtable technique.

However, when the play was over and the cast was taking its bows, Jackson floated into view in a red velvet gown. And she began to cough. And cough.

She coughed the entire time she was onstage for the curtain call, reminding the audience that great actors cannot be expected to silence people who aren't committed to sitting quietly in a theater.

Actors are known to play practical jokes on each other onstage in order to keep the show fresh and also to test the self-control of the victimized actor. But with a play like Martin Dockery's absurdist *A Lonely Monkeyhouse*, one wonders how anything would get stale.

The piece is set in an alternate reality where people possess extra body parts. A World Health Organization bureaucrat is trying to save a crumbling world but runs out of glue to fix all the cracks in the pavement. A monkey writes plays and ignores the man, named T-Rex, in love with her. A trio of men who interrupt the WHO official's project includes an aspiring orthodontist, played by Gary Klavans, who happens to have three hands.

One night, at the Company of Angels theater in Los Angeles, Patrick Gorman, who played T-Rex, decided *A Lonely Monkeyhouse* was not weird enough. In the wings, he sneaked up on Klavans, who was onstage. Klavans's false arm was protruding into the wings. Gorman grabbed hold of his faux arm and hand and refused to let go. Giving a new and less-than-desirable definition to the term "giving a hand," Klavans was forced to perform the whole scene standing in the same spot.

Cathleen Nesbitt's acting career was both long and highly lauded. But by the time she concluded it with her second American tour as Rex Harrison's mother in the musical *My Fair Lady*, she was ninety years old. Understandably, both oars were no longer in the water.

When the revival opened in New Orleans, a chair was provided for her in the wings so that she would not have to walk all the way to the dressing room between scenes. It turned out her frailty was not just physical.

She complained to director Patrick Garland that the changes to the show were not improvements. Garland did not understand what she meant, as nothing had been changed in the book, lyrics, or music.

Later, he learned that Nesbitt was hearing and seeing parts of the show that had long vanished from her faulty memory.

"There's that new song," she complained. "It's terrible. Something about the rain in Spain."

When the tour hit San Francisco, Nesbitt turned ninety, and the media played up this milestone. On her first entrance, the audience gave her a standing ovation.

Confused, Nesbitt gave a graceful curtsy and immediately left the stage. She'd thought it was the curtain call at the end of the show.

To perform in a theater, in any context, is to be exposed. Add being naked and you'll really understand vulnerability.

Bruce Greenwood, who has worked in many of the films of Atom Egoyan, was in Martin Sherman's *Bent* at the Arts Club in Vancouver. He had to perform the following actions in this charming little play about Nazis and homosexuals and death: he would stroll naked onstage in a scene with Alan Gray, go into the bathroom, put on a bathrobe, and return to the conversation, only to have two Nazi goons smash down the door of his apartment and chase him back into the bathroom.

Once in the bathroom of the set, Greenwood filled both cheeks with blood packets and squirted about a cup of fake blood on one of his legs. The brownshirts then fired a prop gun through the door, whereupon Greenwood screamed, burst out of the bathroom, and tried to run again.

The Nazis grabbed him by the hair, dragged him to the center of the stage, and then pulled out a large knife, filled with more stage blood, and appeared to cut his throat. Then Greenwood vomited the blood he had been storing in his mouth and collapsed face-first on the floor.

A curtain with a massive iron bar anchoring it would then fall in front of Greenwood, creating a backdrop for the next scene, while actor Alex Diakun, in drag, would enter stage right singing a torch song.

Being naked onstage, and then being shot, sliced open, and falling face-first would be a tall task for any actor, eight nights a week. But one night, Greenwood had an even more daunting challenge. He had to keep from passing out onstage.

It was just another night at the Arts Club: killer Nazis chasing Greenwood as he ran bloodied from the bathroom. But suddenly the belt to the bathrobe came open as he ran and, before he knew it, the robe flew off him and wrapped around his feet, forcing him to fall, naked, face-first. It happened so quickly he did not even have time to try and break his fall with his hands.

This meant that his forehead and his penis, which had uncooperatively swung over toward his pelvic bone, both smashed onto the stage.

The pain was staggering, and Greenwood feared that his manhood had been torn off in the impact. He staggered to his feet, pain coursing through his head and groin, only to have those two homicidal maniacs grab him and cut his throat once again.

Greenwood fell forward, dying, as was his custom. Unbelievably, his suffering was not over. His position was too far downstage, and the weighted curtain came plummeting down on his neck.

Greenwood's head, wearing a grimace of pain, was still visible under the curtain as Diakun came on dressed as a woman and started singing. Rather than let his bloody head upstage his fellow actor, Greenwood decided his character would come back to life. He wrestled his head out from under the iron bar of the curtain, withdrew into the dark, and found, with some small measure of relief, that his penis was still attached.

There is always an element of danger, a potential for unintended injury, during a staged fight.

That danger increases exponentially when an actor improvises a violent act for the first time and catches other performers off guard.

When *The Trojan Women* was staged at the Long Wharf Theatre in New Haven, one actress playing Cassandra must have thought she was Queen of the Universe. Her frustration during scenes that did not go well often led to a maniacal thrashing of her arms, which often resulted in her smacking anybody within a few feet of her.

David Spielberg, a young actor playing Talthybius, had been the recipient of six or so instantaneous outbursts of corporal punishment from the hair-trigger temper of Cassandra.

It got so bad, he began asking the advice of other actors in the company.

Martin Maguire, Menelaus in the production, gave Spielberg some advice that clearly showed Maguire could have a career as a diplomat:

"Hit the bitch back," he snarled.

Spielberg was too much of a gentleman to verbally or physically attack the crass Cassandra.

But the worst incident of spastic anger was to follow. On another night, the unbalanced, incendiary Cassandra felt herself disconnected from the audience and players, and in the middle of a scene, her arms whipped outward from floor level.

Her hand snapped into Spielberg's face, and he snapped—in his own way. Tasting the blood on his lips, Spielberg immediately turned to two actors dressed as guards.

"Guards, take her away!" He gave a majestic wave of his own arm and, lo, it was done.

And the scene ended at the halfway point, cementing the lesson in Cassandra's mind.

When Beverly Bozeman was twenty-two years old, she was brought in to play across from Ray Bolger in *Where's Charley?* for her first Broadway lead role. Bolger, who played the Scarecrow in the classic film *The Wizard of Oz*, had been Bozeman's idol.

But when Bozeman was cast, she received warnings from other company members. Bolger, who had been in the show for a year already, tended to lose his temper when things were not exactly right onstage. And he was inclined to take it out on the first person who came into view.

For two weeks, Bozeman had no problems. Then, costume designer David Ffolkes came up with a new gown for her, despite Bozeman's satisfaction with her current outfit. The new design could have been described as "ingenue insanity": it was yellow with tulle sleeves, ruffles, and bows for days.

The first time she changed into this wearable yellow wedding cake, Bozeman and the chorus awaited the arrival of Bolger. It was the Red Rose Cotillion, where Bolger danced with Bozeman.

But that night, Bolger was a little late getting onstage. He had just changed from Aunt to Charley in tuxedo and tails and, as he fussed to get his clothes straight, he looked up to see Bozeman in Ffolkes's latest concoction.

Bozeman saw that Bolger was furious at the change in costume, especially since he had not been consulted. And she feared the first person to taste his wrath would be his dancing partner.

Indeed, as Bozeman danced in the unfamiliar dress, Bolger stuck his foot out. Bozeman, as she fell to the stage, could only think of one thing: that the loveable Scarecrow from *The Wizard of Oz* had just purposely tripped her in front of the audience.

She also sensed that if she let Bolger get the better of her now, the rest of the run would be a living hell. So she remained seated on the stage, gesturing with her arms both left and right, so that the audience would think it was all part of the choreography. Fortunately, Bozeman had been working as a choreographer and was able to incorporate the move swiftly and smoothly.

Bolger hissed viciously, "Get up!" Bozeman continued waving her arms about below him. Bolger ordered her again to rise and, this time, Bozeman was ready.

"Not until you give me your hand," she said, meeting his eyes with a cold gaze.

The orchestra continued playing the waltz as Bolger and Bozeman stared hatefully at each other.

Bolger realized the only graceful way he could get out of the situation he had wrought was to bow elegantly and offer Bozeman his hand. As small revenge, Bozeman took her own sweet time taking his hand and rising. They worked their way back into the tempo of the never-ending waltz.

When their eyes met again, Bozeman said the most natural thing she could under the circumstances.

"Don't you ever," she quietly growled, no longer thinking of him as the cute Scarecrow, "do that again to me, you son of a bitch!"

6

Who Asked You?

(Audience-Actor Interaction)

BOB ZMUDA, WHO created so many memorable gags and bits for his comedian pal Andy Kaufman, was given a free ticket to see Richard Burton perform *Equus* on Broadway. Unfortunately, the call from his friend came in around noon; Zmuda had been awake for thirty hours in a row and the show was a two o'clock matinee.

Zmuda was seated onstage as one of twelve "jurors," as stipulated in the text of the courtroom drama. In the front row of this onstage jury box, Zmuda was enchanted by Burton's rich, melodic Welsh accent—so enchanted that he soon fell asleep.

He was awakened by the sound of his own snoring. Richard Burton's apoplectic, red face was inches from his. The entire theater was staring at Zmuda.

"Sorry, Mr. Burton," Zmuda murmured, ashamed. "I haven't slept in two days." Burton, furious, continued to stare hatefully at him. Zmuda then raised his voice and addressed an apology to the entire theater. "Sorry, I haven't slept in a couple days. Sorry." He stood up and left the theater. When he got home, haunted by his recent theatrical nightmare, he still couldn't sleep.

Andy Kaufman was noted for many hoaxes, but one of his biggest nearly turned into a full-scale riot. His alter ego, the obnoxious Las Vegas lounge singer Tony Clifton, who prided himself on insulting and infuriating everyone he came into contact with, was booked by comedian Rodney Dangerfield to be his opening act at Bill Graham's Fillmore West in San Francisco.

There were boos and hisses as Kaufman, disguised as Clifton, merely stood at the edge of the stage. He antagonized the crowd, saying he would not start his show until he had complete quiet among the hundreds and hundreds of Dangerfield fans. Instead, he heard numerous chants of "Rodney! Rodney!" and the ever-popular "Fuck you!"

Fearlessly, he taunted them. "Believe me, people, I got all night."

Clifton/Kaufman finally began his act with a grating, harsh-voiced version of the song "I Left My Heart in San Francisco," which predictably annoyed the crowd even more. After each interruption from the audience, Clifton would stop singing, shout "Shut up!" and go back to the very beginning of the song.

A shower of beer, liquor, and soda bottles poured onto the stage, and Clifton had to duck and cover like a boxer to avoid serious injury.

"I want respect!" he shouted, an allusion to Dangerfield's signature line, "I get no respect." In the wings, Kaufman's writer, Bob Zmuda, their manager, George Shapiro, and Dangerfield himself laughed at the success of the hoax.

Until an old man climbed onto the stage at the Fillmore West and lunged toward Clifton with a pocket knife. Security intercepted him and dragged him away.

Shapiro smiled as he turned to Zmuda. "Great idea," he said, referring to the homicidal man. "When did you hire that plant?"

Zmuda explained the man was not part of the act, that he was an audience member who really wanted to kill Tony Clifton.

The rain of glass bottles continued, so Bill Graham, fearing for Kaufman's safety, brought the curtain down. Clifton had wowed them for approximately three minutes on stage.

The next night, a fishing net large enough to cover the stage was employed for Clifton, who was dressed in San Francisco Police Department riot gear, including a helmet and a microphone attached to his face shield. He was pelted with bottles and fruit and vegetables, but he proudly completed his entire act.

Scottish comedian Billy Connolly was performing for fellow Scottish immigrants in a concert in Brisbane, Australia, and though everyone was from the same country of origin, the material did not translate well.

A few angry Scots jumped up on the stage, demanding their money back. One maniac in a kilt grabbed Connolly's microphone and began making a speech. Another disgruntled patron grabbed the performer's guitar and smashed it to bits. A very large, very angry Scotsman grabbed tour manager Ian Smith, turned him upside down, and repeatedly bashed his head on the stage, as if he were digging a trench.

Connolly, having been knocked down, curled up in a fetal position and pretended to be unconscious. He was later quoted as saying: "They'd have killed me otherwise."

It is not often that a cast mistakes an audience's utter disgust for approval, but that is precisely what happened when Noël Coward's *Sirocco* was performed in London. Apparently, the theatergoers thought actor Ivor Novello was unintentionally funny-looking in blue silk pajamas, and by the time he was kissing actress Frances Doble in act 2, many patrons were cackling with cruel laughter. Some even accompanied lines with grunts and animal noises.

Doble was utterly confused by this response, and by the man in the audience who shouted, "Give the old cow a chance!"

She stopped performing and responded, "Thank you, sir. You are the only gentleman here."

The management, for some inexplicable reason, thought the clamor at the end was approval, and the curtain was raised and lowered for seven minutes on a cast that was completely befuddled. Adding to the confusion, when Doble came out to make her curtain speech, she showed that she had completely misunderstood the audience's temperament.

"Ladies and gentlemen," she announced, "thank you for making this the happiest night of my life."

In a scene that is worthy of a Fellini movie, *The Bard's Banquet* was staged at the Barmera Theatre in Barmera, about 140 miles from Adelaide, Australia. The play is set in the Mermaid Tavern, where literary giants Shakespeare, Marlowe, and Jonson eat a meal onstage, sings songs of the period, and tell the stories of their lives.

The play did not begin until 10:30 P.M. due to the late arrival of the food to be consumed onstage. When the actors began eating the first course—shrimp—some starving audience members shouted out that the food should be shared with the theatergoers. The actor playing Shakespeare asked for quiet and, instead, he received a fusillade of beer cans launched at his head.

When a cooked ox was brought onstage to be devoured by the actors, hunger-inspired lunacy overtook the audience. One man leaped onstage and threw fistfuls of ox to the audience, as if he was feeding wild animals—which, in a sense, he was. Some audience members came up onstage and threw the actors into the seats and got into fistfights over chunks of bread.

One Barmera couple, apparently sexually excited by the turmoil, shouted aloud, "We don't care! We don't care!" They took center stage, and while the riot loomed around them, they began to have sex in full view of everyone.

The closest police station was fifty miles away, so no one interfered with the audience interfering with the production.

John Voysey, an official of the Arts Council of South Australia, which sponsored the tour, was quoted later as saying, "These people do not know what art is. I think Barmera should be bombed flat."

The five hundred businessmen who booked a theater to see a show called *Porno-Erotico* in Catanzaro, Italy, in 1974 were so disappointed by the tameness of the show, they barricaded themselves in the theater for four hours. Catanzaro's unrelenting public prosecutor, Dr. Massimo Bartolomei, had heard about the sexually explicit show and was in attendance that day. He had closed down six theaters and cancelled the screenings of eleven films in the previous eight months, so the producers of *Porno-Erotico* decided to outfox him. They had the cast juggle oranges and sing Neopolitan love songs.

This was acceptable to Bartolomei, but not to the five hundred hardworking, horny businessman who ripped up the seats and blocked the doors, preventing anyone from leaving. It took about one hundred *carabinieri* with machine guns and smoke bombs to end the audience's performance.

The landmark musical *Hair* was produced in the Netherlands by an English producer who was far freakier than any of the hippie characters onstage. He had periodic electro-convulsive therapy whenever his brain required it, powered by an apparatus he kept inside his coat.

Perhaps it was too many jolts of electricity—or not enough—that accounted for the fact that he forgot to actually book a theater for the play. He was reminded of that fact three days before the scheduled opening. He had remembered to invite the Dutch royal family, though, and a circus tent and benches were quickly rented and haphazardly arranged.

Unfortunately, the benches created a seesaw effect when they were sat upon. When the Dutch royal family arrived, all of the audience stood and applauded. The royal family waved and sat down.

The audience then sat down, and the royal family was thrown into the air and dumped unceremoniously into the sawdust.

The band played the national anthem and, as the dignitaries arranged themselves once again on the benches, a group of Dutch creditors arrived to take back the sets, costumes, and lighting, which had not been secured. The show was cancelled.

It is not known if the producer's mobile shock therapy unit functioned properly that evening.

Some plays have closed after one night. The rarity is one that closes after the first act. But surely the shortest run at a major theater occurred on the night of December 26, 1888. Baron Edward Bulwer-Lytton's play *The Lady of Lyons* was scheduled for a revival the day after Christmas at the Shaftesbury Theatre in London.

Bulwer-Lytton got coal in his stocking that year. After waiting for an hour, the audience was told to go home because the safety curtain could not be raised.

The producers decided not to open the show, and *The Lady of Lyons* opened and closed without the curtain ever having risen.

John Gielgud was in *Oedipus* at the National Theatre in London in 1968. Director Peter Brook decided to have, as part of the set, a gigantic golden penis, center stage, thirty feet high.

The night that actress Coral Browne came to the show, she took one look at the phenomenal phallus and declared, "Well, it's no one I know."

George S. Kaufman sent a telegram to one of the leads in his play *Of Thee I Sing.* What makes this notable is that the telegram was sent while the actor was onstage in London. During the interval, William Caxton was handed the Kaufman telegram and read the following words.

"AM WATCHING YOUR PERFORMANCE FROM THE REAR OF THE HOUSE. WISH YOU WERE HERE."

The Abbey Theatre in Dublin has seen its share of riots. After the Easter Rebellion against the British in 1916, Sean O'Casey's *The Plough and the Stars* in 1926 opened old wounds. Part of the audience, incensed by the play's theme and its display of the national flag, stormed the stage. Part of the audience, in favor of the work, attacked the attackers. One woman, attempting to hit one of the attackers by throwing her shoe at him, missed and instead struck an actor onstage.

W. B. Yeats, the senior director of the Abbey at the time, called the police and went onstage, shouting to be heard above the mayhem. He recalled the previous Abbey riot for J. M. Synge's *The Playboy of the Western World,* nineteen years before, and admonished them, "You have disgraced yourselves again; you are rocking the cradle of a new masterpiece."

The police had to be present for the remaining performances.

The riot Yeats was referring to, on January 26, 1907, was on the opening night of Synge's play. Lady Gregory, who was helping Yeats in the management of the Abbey, sent him a telegram after the first act, as he was in Aberdeen, Scotland, at the time.

"PLAY IS A GREAT SUCCESS," it read.

But what a difference a word makes. Two acts later, Lady Gregory's second telegram announced, "PLAY BROKE UP IN DISORDER AT THE WORD 'SHIFT.'"

In fact, the winds of success had shifted. In 1907 Ireland, *shift* referred to a lady's undergarment and was not spoken of in public. At the mention of a petticoat, the theater erupted in shouts and some audience members stormed the stage.

According to William Fay, the lead actor, the only thing preventing a mob from taking over the stage itself was a call boy who ". . . had armed himself with an axe (*sic*) . . . and swore by all the saints in the calendar that he would chop the head off of the first lad who came over the footlights."

The second night went no better. Hisses and boos greeted the production as soon as the curtain went up. Fay, ten minutes into the play, asked the troublemakers to leave the theater, but it was not to be. Police were called in, and some offenders were taken away. But the noise in the Abbey continued throughout, and by the end of that second performance, there were cries of "Kill the author!"

All this because of a reference to a lady's slip? Maybe, maybe not. True, the character of Christy Mahon insists he will marry only Pegeen Flaherty, even if offered "a drift of Mayo girls standing in their shifts itself." And then, a female character pulls off her petticoat to give to Christy. Synge's line was "a drift of chosen females," but Fay changed it to "Mayo girls," making the insult quite specific and prompting the first protester of the week to shout back, "That's not life in the west of Ireland."

But the audience was already uneasy by that point, near play's end. *Playboy of the Western World* also mercilessly lampooned simpleminded Irish country folk, depicting them as gullible and drunken, and also made a joke of the character Christy Mahon's alleged murder of his father.

During the play's one-week run, there were attempts by patrons to jump onstage. Vegetables were thrown at performers. Fistfights erupted inside the theater and inevitably spilled out into the surrounding streets of Dublin. All this, despite the nightly presence of police, who, by week's end, numbered five hundred.

On January 31, the *Irish Independent* newspaper ran an editorial that explained some of the released hostility. That piece suggested it was not so much Synge's work as where it was staged that created havoc: "It was not for the purpose of lessening Ireland's self-respect and holding her people up to the ridicule of the world that the 'National Theatre' was established."

Was this the worst riot in the history of the United Kingdom? Certainly not. In a way, the chaos attending O'Casey and Synge's work at the Abbey was the tail end of theatergoing malfeasance. And it was not confined to Ireland. The "old price" riots at the Theatre in Covent Garden in 1809 put the Abbey shenanigans to shame. London audiences rioted continuously every night for two months to protest theater manager John Philip Kemble raising ticket prices. Pit tickets rose from three shillings, sixpence to four shillings, and the upper tier, previously reserved for public tickets, was converted to boxes sold for three hundred pounds per year.

After about seventy days of protests and police actions, Kemble apologized and returned Covent Garden tickets to their previous prices.

The following season, Kemble tried to lease out half the number of boxes as before in the upper tier. The result was the same: more rioting, and Kemble gave up.

Any time a play asks for audience participation, the theater is taking its life in its hands.

J. M. Barrie's classic *Peter Pan* does this when Peter saves the life of Tinkerbell by asking the youthful members of the audience if they believe in fairies. Shouts of "yes" then serve to resuscitate Tinkerbell.

But when Joan Greenwood was playing Peter in London, Hermione Gingold was in the audience among the children.

When Greenwood asked if the children believed in fairies, among the positive responses came Gingold's rich, theatrical voice resounding through the theater: "*Believe* in them, darling? I *know* hundreds of them."

Before the Public Theater had its current home on Lafayette Street in New York City, before the New York Shakespeare Festival operated out of the Delacorte Theater in Central Park, Joseph Papp ran what was called the Shakespeare Workshop at the East River Amphitheater.

Free theater outside brought many who might never have seen a theatrical production. One such couple was overheard at Papp's production of *Julius Caesar*.

Upon exiting the amphitheater, a wife asked her husband who Caesar was.

"Oh, some guy," explained the husband, putting history into perspective, "who lived at the time they built the Second Temple."

In the late 1970s, playwright Willard Simms had two of his one-act plays performed at the Provincetown Playhouse in Greenwich Village. His then wife had decided to increase attendance for *Good Will Blues* and *Debergerac Boogie* by bringing in twenty to twenty-five young ruffians from a nearby reformatory.

Simms remained in the back of the house during the show and could not help but notice that his actors seemed to be having an off night. The words did not flow, and they often hesitated before speaking.

It was only after the show that he learned that some of the little monsters in attendance had been shooting paper clips via rubber bands at the actors and finding their marks with regularity. No one onstage could tell who was doing the attacking and so they went on, painfully, with the show.

The great Laurette Taylor is known for having brought a certain realism and power to the modern stage. She is, alas, also known for having been stage center at one of England's most unpleasant reactions to an American performance.

The night was April 29, 1920, and Taylor was the lead in J. Hartley Manners's *Peg O' My Heart* at the Garrick Theatre in London. Cries from the audience of "We can't see!" haunted the production early in the first scene. The actors were partially obscured by the scenery, a low-slung interior ceiling, and the shape of the theater. Pennies were thrown onstage to announce displeasure.

Producer Charles B. Cochran, obviously a man of vision, decided to stop the show. But Taylor talked him out of it. Instead, tables and chairs were moved downstage and appreciative attendees called out "That's the ticket" and "We can see all right."

But apparently it wasn't all right, despite the scenic ceiling being pulled away into the flies and Taylor placating the crowd, saying, "You see, the scenery was planned for America, where we do everything on a small scale." This brought laughter and cheers.

But for some inexplicable reason, as act 2 unfolded, the catcalls resumed. "Go back to America," some shouted. "We don't want you here," said others. Others disagreed with these assertions and interrupted the actors with shouts of encouragement, including, "We can see. It's an organized gang."

It may well have been, for in addition to more pennies being thrown, the stage was also showered with pieces of tiling, sneezing powder, and stink bombs, not normally brought along for a night of theater.

Actor Seymour Hicks, upset by the behavior of his fellow patrons, called out, "This is not like England!" Other notable attendees pleaded for order. The American ambassador, John W. Davis, was seen leaving with his party by a side door during the chaos.

Finally, unable to endure the reception any longer, Cochran joined Taylor onstage and groused, "I have not brought this great artist two thousand miles to be subjected to such treatment!"

Taylor rejected the title "artist" but looked up to the gallery, responsible for the barrage. "You shouldn't treat a scrubwoman this way!" Breaking down in tears, she ran off; the curtain came down and the lights went up.

The calls from the audience that a gang had engineered the debacle may well have been true. At some point in the past, actress Peg O'Neill had lost the lead in the play *Paddy, the Next Best Thing* to Taylor. Taylor took the play to London. O'Neill was relegated to Chicago. Rumors abounded that O'Neill's boyfriend had engineered the disastrous reception for one of the stage's greatest performers.

Jeffrey Landman played a snail, among other things, in the children's musical theater production of *A Year with Frog and Toad* by Willie and Robert Reale at the International City Theatre in Long Beach, California. In the plot, Snail is asked to deliver a letter from Frog to Toad, and it takes the course of a year, in the play, to accomplish this.

It is usually a child that speaks out inappropriately during live theater. But Landman was shocked by the response of an adult, who acted like the delivery of the letter was taking a year in real time.

Director Kay Cole had Landman as Snail move very slowly over the course of the evening, crossing the stage and walking agonizingly slowly up and down the aisles of the theater.

Finally, no longer able to bear the suspense, an adult patron shouted at the sluggish Landman, "Just deliver the fucking letter already!"

The New Yorker theater critic Robert Benchley was known for expressing his opinion not only in the pages of that magazine but in the audience, aloud, when he was particularly displeased.

One opening night, Benchley had sat through the first act of a play he did not like. The second act curtain rose. A phone onstage rang and rang. No one came onstage to answer it. Obviously, an actor had missed a cue.

Finally, Benchley stood up and announced, "I believe that's for me," and left the theater as the phone continued to ring.

Benchley once again created a bit of noise during the appropriately named play *The Squall* by Jean Bart at the 48th Street Theatre.

Irritated by the use of pidgin English in the play, Benchley warned his wife that if it continued, he would leave.

Sure enough, a while later, an actress playing a gypsy girl prostrated herself at the feet of another character and said, "Me Nubi. Nubi good girl. Me stay."

"Me Bobby," Benchley declared aloud, rising to his feet. "Bobby bad boy. Bobby go."

Richard Stein produced the 1987 awards program of the Connecticut Commission on the Arts at the Paul Mellon Arts Center at Choate Rosemary Hall School in Wallingford, Connecticut. The event was taped in front of a full house by Connecticut Public Television. And for his efforts, Stein got sued.

The event featured performances by jazz great Dave Brubeck, the Goodspeed Opera House, and Pilobolus Dance Theatre. And then Betty Jones came on, and it all went so very wrong.

Jones, a tall, hefty, imposing mezzo-soprano with the Metropolitan Opera, sang "Barbara Song" from Brecht and Weill's *Threepenny Opera*. After her powerful performance, in keeping with operatic tradition, she took a number of curtain calls, walking into the wings and then back onstage for her bows.

When she finally left the wings to head backstage, the stage manager called for the orchestra pit to descend with the piano her accompanist had played. But Jones felt she could milk one more curtain call from the appreciative audience.

So she turned around and headed back out onstage. Unfortunately, by this time, the pit had descended about eighteen inches. Members of the audience called out with grave concern, "Look out!"

Jones tumbled into the lowered pit. Actor Keir Dullea, cohost for the evening, fished Jones out with the aid of an utterly unnerved Stein and they helped her backstage.

There, Stein's wife found a cooler with ice and beverages, took out the drinks, and plunged Jones's injured foot into the icy waters. To Jones's great credit, she was very apologetic, admitting she should not have gone back for that one extra curtain call.

Perhaps not so much to her credit, after discovering she had broken her ankle, Jones sued Stein and everyone remotely associated with the event.

In the final settlement, the only person Stein had to pay was the person who always benefits from these kinds of incidents: his attorney.

Jones's husband was also a plaintiff in the suit. He filed suit for "loss of conjugal relations."

Corinne Kason was the understudy to Kaye Ballard for the musical *The Barbary Coast* by William Penzner, when it was presented at the Fisher Theatre in Detroit in 1983. She was witness to a bit of blown choreography that made the musical temporarily turn into a punk version of modern dance.

The Barbary Coast is hardly normal to start with. It involves scenes with boxer "Gentleman Jim" Corbett, an opium den, and fight sequences between rival gangs the Red Tongs and the Blue Tongs.

Everyone seemed to be getting along during a dance number in which men interlaced arms with women in a pinwheel effect. The woman dancer on the end of the line would be lifted into the air momentarily, creating a free-floating effect.

In fact, it was a little too free and a little too floating. Three women were tossed into the orchestra pit, altering the music as they crawled off the bodies of musicians and stumbled their way back onto the stage.

Kason, who nearly fell down herself due to the malfunctioning human pinwheel, was also witness to that evening's gang fight between the Tongs. One actor was punched so hard, he lost consciousness and had to be dragged from the stage and taken to the hospital. It must have been one of the few moments in theater history when an understudy prayed not to be given a chance to go on again.

Boca Raton means "mouse's mouth" in Spanish, and it was fitting that John Kander and Fred Ebb's musical *Cabaret* was presented at the Royal Palm Playhouse in Boca Raton, Florida, when a member of the audience was mouthing off.

The staging of *Cabaret* was in the round, and Kris Montgomery, who played the role of Sally Bowles, was in a party sequence one night when she heard a member of the audience complain aloud, "I can't see. Get out of the way."

Montgomery heard this and assumed it was directed at her, but she remained calm and thought to herself that she would be crossing to another area of the stage in a few moments and that that would certainly satisfy the cranky audience member.

After Montgomery moved to the other side of the stage, she took a surreptitious glance out into the stalls, whence the voice had emanated. She then realized the comment had not been meant for her. A man was trying to exit to go to the bathroom and the rather aged patrons in his way were making no effort to let him go by.

As the scene continued, the man with the pressing toilet appointment got louder and more insistent—to no avail. Finally, he took the only route available to him, one that ran onto the stage itself.

As soon as the man entered the lit area of the stage, he knew the audience and players could see him. As a small concession, he kept one foot onstage and one foot in the audience, walking awkwardly on two different levels.

It was at this moment that Moses Terlitzsky, who played Max, the club owner, entered, only to find himself facing a man standing on a slant, his feet at two different heights, in front of the entire audience.

Showing great sensitivity, the man stopped Terlitzsky and asked loudly, "Which way to the bathroom?"

Astounded, Terlitzsky broke character and feebly pointed in the correct direction, and then entered the party scene.

The audience member headed in the right direction. He didn't even say "thank you."

Laurel Ollstein performed in the now defunct San Francisco Shakespeare Company. One night, when the character of Claudio was sentenced to death, the actor's elderly Jewish grandmother, in attendance, loudly proclaimed, "Oy, they're gonna kill Bobby!"

In the history of theater audience chaos, one can cite the occasional argument—even, on a bad day, a fistfight. It is extremely rare, thankfully, to have actual gunfire in the crowd. That sort of thing is currently left to dance clubs.

But at the esteemed Lucille Lortel Theatre in New York, a patron was in fact shot during the waning days of Robert Harling's *Steel Magnolias*. The efforts of Suzy Hunt, who played Truvy, to console the injured party led to a bizarre revelation.

While Hunt was onstage, exchanging lines with another actress, a gun went off in the house and then a groan was heard. An audience member sitting in the front row got up and bolted down the aisle toward the lobby.

"That was a gunshot!" announced Hunt, which was neither her next line nor a surprise to anyone within earshot. Nevertheless, stating the obvious is sometimes absolutely necessary, and the stage manager gathered the entire cast together backstage, temporarily putting a halt to the play.

The stage manager asked the cast if, under the circumstances, they were willing to go on with the performance. The cast agreed to do so, and they began from the top, sailing through the play without even the smallest handgun being discharged.

Hunt, upon learning a woman had been shot in the leg, discovered her name and went to visit her the next day in Saint Vincent's Hospital. She arrived with a bouquet of flowers, but the woman, surrounded by her husband and family, did not seem very welcoming. Puzzled, Hunt presented the flowers, wished her a very speedy recovery, and quickly left.

It was later determined by the police and the box office at the Lucille Lortel why the injured woman acted so uncomfortable in Hunt's presence. Her seat and the one adjoining her had been paid for by a friend, a man with whom she was apparently having an affair. He was packing a gun at the time, and when his coat slipped off his lap during the show, he accidentally shot his lover through the leg.

Performers do not customarily "break the fourth wall" and interact with the audience directly, unless it is improvisational theater or experimental in nature or perhaps a club act or magic show. But there is a type of theater that prides itself on erasing the boundaries between actor and audience. It is known as interactive theater, and it often involves a humorous murder mystery or cultural event.

Reed Kalisher was in one such show, *Grandma Sylvia's Funeral.* Written by Glenn Wein and Amy Blumsack, the piece traveled from Los Angeles to Philadelphia to New York to the Broward Stage Door Theatre in Coral Springs, Florida, where Kalisher had the role of Uncle Harvey, one of poor, dead Sylvia's sons.

The play depicts an amusingly dysfunctional family in mourning. It was staged in the theater and in the lobby. The characters' actions were heavily scripted, but left room for improvising. One night, an improv that no one could have predicted took place.

Grandma Sylvia's Funeral did not have an intermission, per se, but it did have a "mitzvah meal," a table set up with bagels, spreads, drinks, and cookies, all kosher, that the audience could help itself to at any time, so that the interactive action would not be interrupted.

But about two minutes past the midway point of the show, one of the audience members interrupted the show in a big way. He was choking to death on a piece of food.

Now, to create more humor, there was a son-in-law character

who was supposed to be a doctor and had married into the family. He was played by a black actor. He wasn't really a doctor, and he sure as hell wasn't Jewish. But he happened to be sitting near the man turning blue with food stuck in his esophagus. Being the closest, he rushed over to try and help.

Audience members simply lost their sense of logic during this emergency in a most peculiar setting. Acting as if the actor playing a doctor was, in fact, a real doctor, people shouted, "Let the doctor in!" "Get out of the doctor's way!"

Further blurring reality, the black actor-doctor knew the Heimlich maneuver and performed it on the choking patron, helping to dislodge the food and save the man's life.

The show went on, people continued to watch and eat, and, when it was all over, Kalisher heard numerous comments from the crowd to the effect of, "It's a good thing there was a doctor in the house."

There are a fair share of stories of actors who, faced with annoying patrons talking or making noise, break character and harshly reprimand the offender.

But playwright Richard Kramer saw a gentler approach when he went to see Dorothy McGuire in Tennessee Williams's *Night of the Iguana* at New York's Circle in the Square.

A female voice in the crowd, during the play, kept insisting, "I want to see Dorothy McGuire! I want to see Dorothy McGuire!"

It was not clear to McGuire whether the woman had her view of the stage blocked, thought McGuire was actually an understudy for herself, or whether the audience member was simply on drugs or mentally deranged.

Her focus broken for the moment, McGuire turned to the audience and said to the throng, in the cadences of her genteel Southern character, "May I present to you, please, a fellow human being," and returned to the play.

The Independent newspaper in Britain reported in 1987 that a premiere performance of Eugène Ionesco's *Journeys among the Dead,* at the Riverside Studio, was plagued by ". . . an old Frenchman who talked all the way through the first act." The paper went on to report that the dispirited old man left during the interval and turned out to be none other than Ionesco himself.

Director Stuart Wood told the cast that the iconic Theater of the Absurd playwright said to him afterward, "Oh, my God, I have written an awful play. I have let a lot of people down. My life is worthless."

Apparently reassured by the director, Ionesco returned two days later to give it another chance. But Ionesco thought *Journeys* even deader than before. Again, he mumbled disapprovingly and loudly enough to provoke one of the actors to ask Wood to ask Ionesco to keep his voice down.

Woodie Anderson was in the ensemble of the musical *Jesus Christ Superstar* when it was done at the Lorain Palace in Lorain, Ohio. During the sequence of the Andrew Lloyd Webber–Tim Rice musical in which Jesus is given forty lashes, accompanied by crescendoing rock music, one audience member was whipped into a real frenzy.

A man wearing blue jeans and a T-shirt ran onto the stage from the audience and threw his body over actor Mike Larochelle, in the role of Jesus, to protect him from the staged whipping. Larochelle looked very perplexed and so did the two actors playing guards.

But their hesitation was momentary. They were, after all, guards, and so they did what guards do. Short of crucifying the interloper or plunging a spear into him, the guards grabbed him and tossed him down the raked stage, rolling him like a bowling pin into the orchestra pit.

The management of the theater wanted the man arrested but, remarkably, he recovered from his plunge into the pit, picked himself up, ran out an exit, and got away.

When the show was over, the performer playing Judas was extremely concerned about the zealous audience member coming after him. After all, his character had turned Jesus in to the authorities. Judas had to be forced to go onstage to take a curtain call and refused to leave the theater after the show to go to his car without being accompanied by security.

Before heading for his car, the performer who was Judas asked nervously what the man looked like, should he suddenly encounter him in the parking lot.

He was told, "Just look for the guy in the 'White Power' T-shirt."

When the musical *On the Twentieth Century* was performed at the St. James on Broadway in 1978, it won Tony Awards for Best Musical, Best Book of a Musical, Best Original Score, Best Actor and Actress in a Musical, Best Featured Actor and Actress in a Musical, Best Scenic Design and Best Direction of a Musical. The

Cy Coleman/Betty Comden/Adolph Green musical also garnered five Drama Desk awards.

It would seem that all this talent, pulled together into one great production, was just too much for two patrons to handle. Sal Mistretta, who played two small character roles in the ensemble, recalled seeing a woman in the first row of the St. James giving her boyfriend what is colloquially referred to as a "hand job" during the show.

Mistretta also remembers, after the completion of that act, the next song performed was the optimistically titled "I Rise Again."

Steve Moore spent much of his stand-up comedy career doing material that avoided the fact that he is gay. It was at the Comedy Store in La Jolla, California, that he was "outed" by a loud, obnoxious, drunken audience member. But Moore had the last laugh, as stand-ups usually do.

It was the third show on a Saturday night, when crowds are the most unruly. Moore was flying high, getting laughs in all the right places, joking with the audience, playing Led Zeppelin songs on his accordion.

A Southerner by birth, Moore asked the responsive crowd, "Anyone out there from the South?"

Suddenly, the dream performance was ruptured by a drunkard who bellowed crudely, "On your knees, faggot!"

Without missing a beat, Moore shot back, "How about the North?"

Comedic actor Bill Murray got his start with the Second City troupe in Toronto. Murray's smooth, laid-back style, which many have come to admire, was not on display one night at the Old Firehall Theatre, where he was heckled relentlessly by one idiotic patron.

Second City alumnus Robin McCulloch recalled the night well, especially when the heckler continued his insults during a request for suggestions in an improvisation set.

Murray had had enough. "Fuck you and your date, too!" he screamed. Then he jumped off the stage, grabbed the man, dragged him outside, and, according to McCulloch, "reinvented the angle at which his arm should bend."

Theater patrons deserve to be taken out of the theater when they speak aloud or try to interact with the performers. But what about when they laugh too much? And for the wrong reason?

Daniel Noah and a friend were truly excited about seeing director Robert Woodruff's daring staging of *The Changeling*, a Jacobean theater classic by Thomas Middleton and William Rowley. But when the lights went down at the St. Clement's Church Theatre in New York, Noah and his friend were astonished. Woodruff had directed the cast to slither along the walls of the set with grand, exaggerated, flamenco dance movements. They delivered their lines in booming, histrionic voices.

The audience sat rapt, with the exception of Noah and his friend, who suddenly found themselves laughing, slightly at first, and then after a while so uncontrollably that they shook their seats. They were the only ones laughing in the theater and began to unintentionally annoy other patrons.

During intermission, the two giddy theatergoers calmed themselves down. But when they returned to their seats, a brave man, on behalf of a group of resentful patrons, asked them to not stay for the second act.

Although they meant no disrespect to the renowned Woodruff or anybody else, they realized that the laughter might start all over again and they agreed to leave.

Sometimes the show must be temporarily stopped for an emergency. But it is rare when, after doing so, the performers decide the show must not go on. And it's almost unheard-of for a performer to be commended for refusing to continue.

Steve Bluestein was doing his stand-up comedy act, opening for singer Barry Manilow at the Riviera Hotel in Las Vegas, at the height of Manilow's popularity. Bluestein was about nineteen minutes into his act, the midpoint, in front of a jammed room of customers, when a man screamed out, "I need a doctor!"

Bluestein looked down into the crowd and saw a woman having a seizure. The house lights went up and paramedics arrived, put her on a stretcher, and took her away.

The house lights went out again, and a spotlight came up on Bluestein, whom the crowd expected to instantly make them laugh again.

Bluestein looked out into the darkened house, leaned into the microphone, and said, "I don't think comedy is appropriate right now." He had no idea how the audience would react.

He received thunderous applause as he walked offstage.

To their credit, critics commended him for his actions.

The next day, while sitting in a coffee shop, Bluestein saw the same woman, looking perfectly fine.

"Remember me?" she asked the stunned Bluestein. "I was at the show last night." She added, helpfully, "I was the one who had the seizure."

Garry Marshall, after working as a director, producer, and actor in television and film, opened the Falcon Theatre in Burbank, a 130-seat space that often puts on children's theater during the weekends, introducing kids to live theater often for the first time.

One afternoon, *Sleeping Beauty* was being presented, and the actor playing Prince Charming entered wearing very close-fitting tights.

A young boy in the front row, who could not have been much more than four years old, clearly was having his first live theater experience. He stood up and, clear as a bell, announced to his mother and the rest of the Falcon Theatre, "Mommy, I can see Prince Charming's penis!"

Larry Dean Harris has written his share of plays, but he was also one of the actors in the Toledo Repertoire Theatre production of *Pump Boys and Dinettes*. The show, which has played all over the world, was conceived and written by John Foley, Mark Hardwick, Debra Monk, Cass Morgan, John Schimmel, and Jim Wann.

Harris had been given a lot of freedom to ad-lib during the run. At one performance, it became clear that there were plumbing problems in the bathrooms. People had been complaining, and so, rather than ignore the problem, Harris decided to make light of it from the stage.

"All right," Harris suggested in a good-natured Western twang, "everybody cross their left leg and look at the bottom of your neighbor's shoe." The improv got a big laugh.

The major exception was a man seated in the back of the house who had a terrified look on his face and forced his way out of his aisle and out of the theater.

Harris learned later that the man's colostomy bag had broken.

Jordan Baker played the character C in Edward Albee's *Three Tall Women* at the Promenade Theatre in New York. And even though it garnered a Pulitzer Prize for drama, not everything went swimmingly every night.

Just before one opening curtain, the stage manager told Baker and the two other women in the cast that Al Pacino was in the audience. Suddenly, the energy for that show went up a few notches.

Ten minutes into the play, Baker was seated on a chair, facing sideways, when she heard an annoying "ping" sound every thirty seconds or so. The pings started to occur more frequently, and Baker could not identify what they were.

Under equity rules in the United States, no matter what is happening in the audience, actors must continue to perform until a stage manager makes the announcement, "Actors to the greenroom," indicating they should wait backstage until a decision is made about continuing the show. This rule has a great deal to do with the fact that the theater box office has to return money to patrons if a performance is halted in the first act.

So the "three tall women," portraying different stages of life of the same character, kept performing, despite the sound of louder and louder pings, and then rustling noises, and cries of "Oh, no!" and "Move! Move!" On they played, even though people in the audience began standing up suddenly and crawling over seats. The actresses had no idea what was happening and were in no position to ask.

Finally, the announcement was heard. "Actors to the greenroom," came a voice over the speakers in the Promenade, and the play was stopped. The house lights came on. Baker looked out into the audience and screamed, "Oh, my God!"

A water pipe had burst in the upstairs apartment complex. The orchestra section of the theater had been turned into a lake.

Backstage, the stage manager told the three women that the leak had started small, with a drop of water landing on a seat, going *ping, ping.*

It was the seat reserved for Al Pacino, who'd never arrived.

During another performance of *Three Tall Women,* Baker was delivering a very sensitive monologue in the beginning of the second act detailing her character's first sexual encounter in 1926.

While she was performing, she noticed, among a few empty rows in the balcony, a woman waving her hand at Baker. This prompted Baker to wonder who the person was, how she knew her, and whether she expected Baker to stop her monologue, squint into the lights, recognize the person, and say, "Hey, how are you? Thanks for coming to the show," only to return to her account of being deflowered.

The woman stopped waving and disappeared from sight. But Baker's focus was again challenged some minutes later, this time by two paramedics in white suits who brought a gurney into the balcony and rolled the woman away.

After the show, the stage manager assured Baker that the woman was all right and that she wasn't a friend of Baker's trying to be recognized. Instead, the woman was a diabetic trying to get the attention of her nurse, who started out sitting next to her and then took a better seat a few rows ahead.

When playwright Elyzabeth Gregory Wilder was a resident at the MacDowell Colony in Peterborough, New Hampshire, she had the pleasure of hearing a classic don't-stop-the-show story from director James Lapine.

During a Broadway preview of Stephen Sondheim's *Passion*, Lapine recounted, a woman sitting in front of him was complaining about how awful she thought the musical was. Of course, she had no idea the man who had written the book and directed it was right behind her. She kept complaining to the person next to her and, about halfway through, Lapine lost his patience. He stood up and told the woman that if she didn't like the show, she should leave, and he added a passionate profanity or two in the process.

Lapine enjoyed the rest of the show in peace.

Wilder herself experienced some outrageous events when she worked in New York as an usher, putting herself through college. She was assigned to work the orchestra section during the intermission of *Cats* at the Winter Garden. As the lights flashed, indicating the second act was about to begin, the patrons began to return to their seats. The costumed "cats" began to make their way back onstage, one by one.

Suddenly, Wilder noticed a woman in the audience trying to climb up onto the stage. Wilder quickly approached her and asked her to step away from the stage. But then she saw that it was not a theatergoer but a homeless woman who had wandered into the theater through the open doors at intermission. She wore a worn dress and tattered sweater, and her dirty hair sported several rainbow-colored barrettes in the shape of butterflies.

The homeless woman pushed Wilder away and climbed up onto the stage. The "cats" looked at Wilder, who returned their stunned gazes. The homeless woman began petting the actors, made up to look like cats, and she even began singing an off-key version of the showstopper "Memories."

The house manager in the rear of the theater began screaming for security. The homeless woman, realizing she was meant to be an ensemble player, not the lead, slipped out a side exit and was never caught.

One of the rudest, most revolting actions taken by a paying customer during a Broadway show was also witnessed by Wilder. She must have just been lucky.

Michael Frayn's brilliant, complex psychological thriller about the creation of the atomic bomb, *Copenhagen,* featured a set with seats onstage that were accessible only via the backstage area.

At each performance, an usher was stationed on each side of the onstage seating area to make sure no patron interfered with the action.

It was the night that an usher fell asleep that an irate onstage audience member, who clearly could not follow the action of the play, came down from his seat and walked across the stage at the Royale. He handed his ticket to the startled Philip Bosco, declared *Copenhagen* was "the biggest piece of shit I've ever seen," and exited through the audience.

If ever there was a case crying for police brutality, that was it.

Merle Debusky handled the press for *How to Succeed in Business Without Really Trying* at the 46th Street Theatre in New York. Even more nerve-wracking than opening night of this legendary musical was the performance attended by newly elected President John F. Kennedy, with a phalanx of Secret Service agents.

For this Frank Loesser musical, during the number "Coffee Break," director Abe Burrows had one of the office workers, in need of coffee, stumble to the front of the stage and, desperate for a caffeine fix, throw himself into the orchestra at the end of the song.

Minutes before the show started, with the president and some of the agents sitting in the front of the house, Debusky remembered this bit of business and suddenly realized the Secret Service might interpret it as a threat to the president and gun down the poor performer before he even hit the pit.

Debusky ran to a few Secret Service agents, desperately explaining his fears, but they acted like he was some kind of lunatic.

Finally, Debusky found the captain of the unit, who, wide-eyed, agreed it was definitely a potential nightmare. Walkie-talkies crackled across the theater, warning the agents of the swan dive early in the first act.

Thus, Debusky circumvented the first public shooting of a dancer on Broadway by federal agents.

Late one night in 1865, President Abraham Lincoln had a disturbing dream.

He dreamed he was walking through a silent White House at

night and heard sobbing. He entered the East Room and was startled by the sight of a catafalque, a platform upon which was a coffin. It was covered in black and surrounded by mourners.

In the dream, Lincoln asked the guard on duty who had died.

"The president," was his reply.

One week later, Lincoln went to Ford's Theatre in Washington, D.C., and was assassinated by the actor John Wilkes Booth.

Catcalls are understood today to be expressions of impatience or disapproval from those attending live events.

But the origin of catcalls may well be whistling to send a message of objection, and in ancient Greece, both Plato and Demosthenes wrote of the dangers of catcalls for both actors and orators of the time.

Cicero, in ancient Rome, wrote a letter to Atticus in 61 BC boasting that Cicero's oratory was so well-received that he heard ovations "without a single shepherd's whistle (*sine ulla pastoricia fistula*)."

The actual word "catcall" is supposed to have been first written in 1659, in an England considerably less polite than the one we know. In the seventeenth century, a catcall was an instrument. It was a small, circular whistle made up of two plates of tin, with a hole in the center, and was blown mostly during less-than-joyous moments in the English music hall.

There comes a time in live theater when what goes on in the audience and lobby is more interesting than what is presented on the stage.

Lissa Ferreira is the Executive Director of Theatre in the Mountains, nestled in the Santa Cruz Mountains in Los Gatos, California. Her theater was presenting a musical called *Necklace* that had been created by local writers and was, in her opinion, less than satisfactory.

One night, sitting in the audience with her husband, wondering why she had agreed to stage the musical before her, Ferreira saw a woman sit in the row in front of her and bitterly complain about the warmth of the theater. She had brought in a bag of ice and it sloshed noisily around as she moved it about her head and face, disturbing everyone sitting in her vicinity.

Ferreira, as executive director, took executive action. She leaned forward and whispered into the ice-bag lady's ear, "Ma'am, that is really loud and distracting."

The woman, later revealed to be Sandi Nelson by name, whipped her head around and snapped back, "I have a violent headache." Ironically, it would soon be Ferreira who had the worse headache for suggesting Nelson sit in the back of the theater.

Nelson whirled and hit Ferreira in the face with her hand; the large ring she wore cut open Ferreira's lip.

Ferreira ran out to the lobby, where she found a female board member of Theatre in the Mountains and insisted Nelson be removed from the theater. This board member, afraid the unbalanced woman with the ice-bag and frisky hands might attack her, too, suggested that they wait until intermission and then get an apology out of her.

At intermission, a male board member of Theatre in the Mountains arrived in the lobby and was told by the female board member what had happened. He was asked to sternly evict "the woman in pink."

The male board member agreed, but he approached the first woman dressed in pink that he saw, and she was *not* the woman who'd attacked Ferreira.

The board member strode up to the innocent woman and, with danger in his eyes, growled, "You need to step outside or we are going to call the sheriff."

This accusation brought an angry response not only from the innocent woman's husband, who sprang to her defense and yelled at the mistaken board member, but from Nelson, who was standing nearby and overheard. Nelson then began to argue with the board member. Ferreira and the others entered the argument in the lobby and, finally, Nelson, realizing she could be charged with a crime, apologized, saying she would never hurt anyone, even though she just had.

Nelson was offered a seat in a "cooler" section of the theater. As she headed toward it for the beginning of the second act, Nelson turned to Ferreira and viciously hissed, "Yes, I'm sure you would love it if I sat in the back."

Adding insult to injury, Nelson convinced the wife of the musical director to write a letter to the entire board of directors, accusing Ferreira of starting the problem. Ferreira never filed suit against Nelson.

She is still Executive Director of Theatre in the Mountains and has a tiny scar on her lip from where Nelson's ring struck her. One can only hope Nelson still has the violent headache.

Comedian, writer, and actress Carrie Snow once found herself performing at a benefit for the American Cancer Society in a hotel in Boca Raton, Florida.

While she was doing her routine, some drunken and unappreciative male member of the audience walked right up to her and whispered in her ear, "I'll donate $5,000 if you walk off the stage right now without saying another word."

Snow, stunned, walked offstage to a kitchen area, where she burst into tears. The promoter, when told what had happened, accompanied Snow back in front of the audience.

The man had fled, and when Snow continued with the show, she told the audience what the man had whispered in her ear.

Five people immediately volunteered to write checks for $1,000 each.

Producer Joseph Papp did battle with Parks Commissioner Robert Moses over the right to perform plays in New York City's Central Park. Eventually Papp won out, and his production of *Romeo and Juliet* began its citywide tour.

First stop was the amphitheater in Corlears Hook Park. Jerry Stiller recalled that the audience was primarily black and Latino, and much more vocal than a typical theater audience.

When Bryarly Lee recited to Stephen Joyce one of the most famous lines in drama, "Romeo, Romeo, wherefore art thou Romeo," the response came from a member of the audience.

"Give it to her, Pepito! Give it to her good!"

In the old days, when an actor "dried" or "went up" on his lines, there was a prompter offstage or in the orchestra pit to help. But there was no such luck when Ray Bolger completely lost his way in the very first preview of *Where's Charley?* on Broadway.

The Frank Loesser musical has a rather long number, "Once in Love with Amy," that interspersed dancing and singing. It was after the first chorus and some dancing that Bolger suddenly forgot Loesser's words and came to a dead stop—as did the musical.

"Ladies and gentlemen," Bolger admitted to the throng, "I forgot the words. Does anybody here know the words to this song?"

As if on cue, the voice of a young child responded from the dark. "I do, Ray."

Bolger stared out into the lights, unable to see but desperate for help. He asked the child to sing along with him.

"Oh, once in love with Amy / Always in love with Amy," sang the child from his seat. Soon Bolger remembered the lines, the music started up again, and the show ran straight through to the finish.

Afterward, in his dressing room, however, Bolger was clearly embarrassed and covered it up with hostility. "Kids screwing up my number! Why the hell do they let kids in the theater in the first place?"

And in the deafening silence that fell in that dressing room after his outburst, Bobby Loesser, the lyricist's seven-year-old son, stepped forward and said quietly, "It was me, Ray."

The younger Loesser had listened over and over to demo records of the show until he had memorized the whole thing.

Nonplussed, Bolger spluttered, "Shit." Then he cheerfully suggested, "We were really good out there."

On another night, Bolger recalled his duet with Bobby and went to music director Cy Feuer and said, "The audience really liked that. Maybe I should try something like that tonight."

Later in the run, Bolger did just that. He broke out of his solo performance of "Once in Love with Amy" and created a sing-along with the audience.

The reviews of *Where's Charley?* were generally bad.

But, aided in part by Bobby Loesser, the show was a popular success and ran for three years.

When things go wrong onstage, it is often difficult to know whether to be mortified or to laugh.

Peter Ustinov took his young daughter to her first opera, Giuseppe Verdi's *Aida,* at the Baths of Caracalla in Rome. During a major scene, several live animals, including elephants, horses, camels, and stray cats, relieved themselves onstage.

Ustinov felt a tap on his arm. He leaned over so his daughter could whisper in his ear.

"Daddy," she asked most politely, "is it all right if I laugh?"

Not all children are so well behaved in the theater.

One of J. M. Barrie's favorite stories about the London production of his book-turned-musical *Peter Pan* concerned a young boy to whom Barrie had given a free ticket. In fact, the boy was seated in the author's box in the theater.

Afterward, Barrie asked the boy which part he'd liked best.

"What I think I liked best," mused the boy, "was tearing up the program and dropping the bits on people's heads."

In January 1995, the Leeds Playhouse in England staged the world premiere of the play *The Winter Guest* by Sharman McDonald, directed by Alan Rickman. It was about a community cut off by a blizzard and their struggles to survive.

A snowstorm hit Leeds. It was so severe that the snowbound audience had to be put up for the night inside the theater.

The good news about experimental theater is that it is often so extraordinary, audience members cannot tell when things go wrong. The bad news is that audience members sometimes forget the boundaries between player and playgoer.

Richard Schechner directed the landmark production of *Dionysus in 69* for his company The Performance Group in New York. During the performance, which involved audience participation, the character of Pentheus, played by William Shepherd, was customarily sacrificed to Dionysus, a role performed by Jason Bosseau.

One night, a group of Queens College students in attendance physically kidnapped the character of Pentheus to prevent his death in the play. Bosseau, furious at the interruption, jumped between the students carrying Shepherd and the door to the theater, preventing their exit.

Bosseau accused the students of orchestrating a plot to disrupt *Dionysus in 69*. "You came here with a plan worked out!" he shouted at the students.

They agreed, and, moved by the anarchic spirit of the show, they replied, "Why not?"

Before they could carry off Shepherd and change the direction of the piece, an argument ensued. Some members of the audience could not tell whether this change was actually part of *Dionysus in 69* or not.

That question was answered when Shepherd was carried outside the theater and unceremoniously dumped onto Grand Street.

Shepherd, furious about the incident, refused to go back to the performance that night. "I was taken out of it and that's that," he announced as he left.

That still left the performers and most of the audience, waiting to see what one of the most experimental theaters in the United States would come up with next. Bosseau went upstairs and told all to Schechner, who came down and asked for a volunteer from the audience to play the role of Pentheus.

A sixteen-year-old boy who had seen the show five times offered his services. With instructions from the performers and Schechner, as well as his own improvised lines, the play was completed.

This, however, was not the only time that the audience shaped *Dionysus in 69* beyond the parameters set by Schechner. The show had what was called a "Birth Ritual," during which audience members would sometimes stand up, uninvited, and make denunciations of the Vietnam War. During one particular Birth Ritual, a young male model, wearing nothing but a jockstrap, stood up and danced and later handed out business cards with his name and phone number.

In what was known as the "Death Ritual," members of The Performance Group, in threes and fours, would select an audience member and caress that person. This action was taken from a theater workshop exercise, but this too got out of control. Both straight and gay male audience members sometimes touched male and female performers in inappropriate places. In fact, stirred into a frenzy on some nights, audience members groped other audience members. Female members of The Performance Group particularly complained about the caress mess.

As the production went on, the Death Ritual eventually

evolved into a group of naked performers lying in a mass onstage, even though the piece had not originally been staged that way. Not surprisingly, on some nights at *Dionysus in 69*, audience members would strip off their own clothing and join the assembly of flesh.

While the show broke many conventions and stirred much interest in the theater community, it inevitably came to an end, expedited by members of Schechner's Group who were tired of the intrusiveness of audience participation.

When is a rude theatergoer who interferes with a production not a rude theatergoer? When the producer of a failing show has paid that person to cause a ruckus.

Maverick producer David Merrick, noted for his publicity stunts, came up with his most outrageous machination during the New York run of John Osborne's *Look Back in Anger*. While the play changed the history of British theater, the American version of philandering, furious Jimmy Porter did not do well, and ticket sales had dropped off dramatically.

So for $250 Merrick hired a woman to sit in the second row and, at an agreed-upon moment, jump up onstage and physically attack actor Kenneth Haig, playing Porter, ostensibly because the character was cheating on his wife.

As Merrick had hoped, the newspapers reported the incident, assuming it was real and spontaneous. According to Merrick, it extended the life of the play in New York by seven months.

Peter Bull was Pozzo in the Peter Hall production of Beckett's *Waiting for Godot.* The first English-language production of the play, it premiered at the Arts Theatre in London in 1955 and it was a puzzlement to many people who saw it. Bull's own mother showed up at a matinee with an elderly lady friend and even his own dear mum was hard-pressed to find something nice to say to her son.

Finally, Lady Bull managed, "Gladys thought the brasswork in the stalls was beautifully polished."

Early audiences certainly did not fully appreciate what Beckett was doing, and there were cries aloud from the gallery of "Rubbish!" and "Disgusting!" and "It's a disgrace!" At one particular performance, this Theater of the Absurd transformed into Audience of the Absurd, as a fight broke out and someone shouted the epithet, "Balls!"

Hugh Burden and Peter Woodthorpe played the tramps Vladimir and Estragon, and after one exchange, when one character announced, "I'm happy," and the other replied, "I'm happy, too," a third comment came from Row F, where an attendee responded, "Well, I'm bloody well not." The unfulfilled patron then turned to the rest of the crowd and said, "Nor are you. You've been hoaxed, like me."

Burden, which would have been a better name for the loud-mouth, ad-libbed, "I think it's Godot." Some chuckles helped restore the peace and the play went on, and has gone on, to be considered by theater academics as the most important play of the twentieth century, whether you bloody well like it or not.

Someone Like You is a musical that starred Petula Clark and played at the Strand Theatre in London for a single night in 1990. Clark's disappointment at the short run was all the more poignant as she had also written the musical score.

Near the climax of the show, Clark's character confronted her worthless husband in front of a group of American Civil War soldiers. She picked up a rifle and prepared to shoot him dead. The husband stuck his chest out proudly and defiantly and told the concerned troops, "Don't worry. She won't shoot."

From the crowd, a less-than-impressed audience member quietly responded, "She mi-ight!"

Audiences, when they are moved by a performance, will leap to their feet and applaud. Audiences, when they are repulsed, will leap to their feet and rush the stage.

While nearing completion of this collection, this author was notified, in February 2006, of a version of Shakespeare's *Titus Andronicus*, titled *Die Schändung* (*The Violation*) staged by Botho Strauss at the Berliner Ensemble, which Bertolt Brecht founded in 1949. The original version certainly is no day at the fair. In it, Titus's daughter, Lavinia, is raped, her hands are cut off, and her tongue is ripped out.

But rather than finding a more representational way of displaying them, the gory, realistic depiction of these acts onstage stirred German theatergoers at one performance to storm the stage and yell at the performers: "Nazi theater!" Others, referring to the level of violence in the production, shrieked, "You're getting off on it!"

Security guards held the protesters back, and no fewer than thirty members of the audience left the theater immediately.

Artistic director Claus Peymann contended he had not seen such a strong reaction in the theater since the 1960s. The thirty irate refugees from the Berliner Ensemble did not stay to see Tamora, Queen of the Goths, who'd encouraged her sons to rape Lavinia, tricked into eating her sons in the form of a pie, at it is in the end of both the Bard's and Strauss's works.

"Our version begins with Shakespeare," contended Peymann, "but then changes into a modern play. We do have a pie, though," he added, seeming to miss the point about graphic violence onstage.

John Philip Kemble knew that, even in the finest theaters in the West End, you could expect some audience member to eventually open his or her mouth. Certainly it was true in 1779, when he was performing in *Zenobia* at the Drury Lane and a woman seated in a box seat spat out numerous insults at him and his leading lady, Mrs. Mason.

Finally, wishing the woman was in a box underground, Kemble took his case to the audience, who of course wished for the play to continue.

"I am ready to proceed with the play," Kemble offered, "as soon as *that* lady has finished her conversation, which I perceive my continuing with the tragedy is but interrupting."

The rude woman was immediately escorted out of the theater.

This same elegant form of denunciation worked for Kemble during a performance regularly interrupted by the crying of a baby in the stalls.

"Ladies and gentlemen," Kemble announced, halting the action onstage, "unless the play is stopped, the child cannot possibly go on."

Comedian Dave Chappelle found it hard to respond to a heckler one night. It was difficult to spot the person, no doubt because Chappelle was performing not in a comedy club but in New York's Madison Square Garden.

So, rather than trying to respond to someone he could not see, Chappelle asked for help from his many fans.

He told those around the heckler to punch him in the kidneys.

During one of the many musical revues Beatrice Lillie did on Broadway, lyricist Howard Dietz decided to have a little fun on the closing night of a long run.

He filled the first row with his friends, and during her last number, they all put on different-colored beards.

The normally unflappable Lillie was so flustered when she saw all that multicolored facial hair on both sexes that she dashed off to her dressing room.

But to her credit, by the time she got there, she had recovered her good humor.

"Nobody can appreciate my voice anyway," she mused. "I never sing above a whisker."

John Mills and John Gielgud were in Brighton, doing a pre-London tour of the Charles Wood play *Veterans*.

The Brighton audience was not used to hearing coarse language onstage and one man stood up and shouted that the two knights should be ashamed for associating themselves with such filth. He dragged his wife by the hand down the row in an effort to avoid any further expletives.

When he reached the seated Mary Hayley Bell, also known as Lady Mills, John's wife, the man showed how discreet Brightonians could be.

"Out of my fucking way!" he shouted.

When the fervor to get tickets to *My Fair Lady* at the Drury Lane was at its height, the house manager one night noticed a lady with an open seat next to her. He asked if it belonged to her.

She sadly admitted, "My husband was coming but he was killed in a car accident."

The manager expressed his sympathy and asked why she had not invited a family member or friend to join her at the very popular musical.

The woman insisted she couldn't. "You see, they're all at the funeral."

Not all those who interfere with the actors are audience members. One was, quite notably, a former actor.

Susanna Mountfort was a very successful seventeenth-century stage performer in England. One of her greatest roles was that of Ophelia. Regrettably, later in life, Mountfort went mad and had to be supervised night and day.

When it was announced that *Hamlet* was being remounted in London, Mountfort escaped her caregivers and hid in the theater. During Ophelia's big scene, when she goes mad, Mountfort leaped onstage, startling the young woman who was currently playing the role.

The emotion in the theater, though great, could not compare with that within Mountfort. She died shortly thereafter.

Aileen Taylor-Smith was in a production of *Bus Stop* with a young Donald Sutherland in Gravenhurst, Ontario. Neither of them knew Taylor-Smith's young son was in the audience for the first time.

When Sutherland, as the handsome, virile rodeo cowboy Bo Decker, tossed Taylor-Smith as Cherie over his shoulder and carried her offstage, a young boy's voice cut through the air of the theater.

"What's that man going to do with my mommy?"

It is not clear whether the boy understood what William Inge had in mind. Perhaps it is best if he didn't.

There is a love-hate relationship between theaters and critics. Theaters love critics when they love the show, and hate them when they hate it.

The Public Theater's Joseph Papp had a feud with Edith Oliver of *The New Yorker* over a review she wrote with which he vehemently disagreed. Oliver received a letter indicating she was "disinvited" from future performances at the Public.

It must be remembered, above all things, that theater critics do love theater. Oliver went and paid to see some Beckett plays at the Public and, knowing she was not welcomed by Papp, she crouched in the back of the theater.

Papp happened to notice her and approached her.

"Why don't you sit in front, where there are empty seats?"

Astonished, Oliver mumbled, "Well, I thought you were furious at me and . . ."

"Furious?" objected Papp. "But that was three days ago!"

Not all interruptions on the part of an audience member are unwelcome.

Melody Ryane was one of three actresses playing cheerleaders in Jack Heifner's *Vanities*. At the Stage West Theatre in Winnipeg, Manitoba, they had decided, instead of using wooden blocks, as suggested in the play, to have the performers stand on Plexiglas cubes.

When Ryane joined two other actresses in a cheer, opening the second-night performance, her legs crashed through the cube and pitched her forward, face-first, onto the stage.

Like most actors, she refused to let this stop her. Ryane got right back up and continued her cheer as if nothing had happened. When she glanced over at the other two actresses in cheerleader outfits, they looked drained of blood. It was then that Ryane looked down and saw blood gushing out of both of her legs.

A nurse stood up in the audience and declared, "You have to stop!" She marched up onstage and surveyed the damage and it was decided that Mary Long, the second cheerleader, would take Melody to the hospital.

The third cheerleader, Lorna Patterson, entertained the audience for two hours.

The crowd in Winnipeg really got its money's worth that night. For Ryane returned, with fourteen stitches in her right leg and, still in shock and not feeling the pain, she and the cast proceeded to do the entire show.

Katharine Hepburn was not in the habit of performing in musicals. And after one night in Cleveland, on tour with *Coco* by André Previn and Alan Jay Lerner, she certainly lost the will to do another.

Coco told the life of famed designer Coco Chanel. On the night in question, a camera flashbulb went off in the audience. Incensed, Hepburn stopped performing and furiously stared out at the audience.

"Who the hell did that?" she demanded to know.

A nervous girl admitted to the indiscretion.

"If you had any guts," Hepburn stormed, "you would leave." The young girl, though mortified, did not move.

"If we don't have regard for each other," Hepburn raged on, "it will be the end of us."

With that, she apologized to the rest of the house, and the scene continued.

Critics generally considered Hepburn's performance in *Coco* to range from weak to deplorable.

For a male stand-up comedian, there is only one indignity worse than having a man in the audience come up and beat you senseless onstage. And that's having a woman do it.

In 1979 Mark Breslin was part of a group of comedians who were booked in a strange variety of venues, ranging from jazz clubs to biker bars. They began in a seedy little dive in Calgary, a strip joint by day and a heavy metal music club by night. Why comedy was booked there is anyone's guess.

The first of three nights was like performing in a mausoleum. There was no reaction whatsoever to the jokes. The comedians assumed they would have an easier crowd on the second of their three nights there.

They never got to the second night. At 3 A.M., a hotel employee pounded on Breslin's door and brought him down to the manager, who informed him that his group of comedians was not funny and that they all had to vacate the premises immediately.

Breslin pulled out the contract they had signed. The manager pulled out a large gun from a drawer and said, "This is my contract."

Twenty minutes later, the funny guys were outside in -30° F weather, looking for a place to stay.

The next stop was at a rock venue in the suburbs of Vancouver. Once again, their representative had not done his homework. It was assumed Breslin and company were male strippers.

That night, they performed their jokes in front of "lady bikers" who wanted to see male flesh, not hear jokes. Breslin came out to open the show and introduce the comedians. Before he could leave the stage for the first act, a lady biker got up onstage and knocked him unconscious with one punch.

When Breslin regained consciousness, he was in a hospital and learned that the women bikers had torn the place apart and a group of police had to break up the riot.

When a stand-up comedian really makes an audience laugh, it is said he or she really "killed." But one night Shawn Alex Thompson, performing in a United Nations-controlled zone in Cyprus, was almost the one killed.

The variety show he was performing for the Canadian Armed

Forces was on the Green Line, a zone in Cyprus only UN forces could enter due to hostility between Greece and Turkey. In fact, days before Thompson's arrival, a Greek guard had shot and killed a Turkish guard, reportedly by accident. By the time Thompson and the show arrived, the tension in Cyprus was almost unbearable.

The show was held in a former five-star hotel that had been badly shelled and was now used for Canadian barracks. There were two nights of shows scheduled in the cavernous, war-damaged hotel ballroom. In order to please everyone, the Turkish general had been invited for the first night and the Greek general for the second.

With no restrictions on material, Thompson figured soldiers would like jokes about war. To open the night, he used a bit that had gone over well in North America. He told the crowd how much they were going to like the performers and then pulled out a handgun that shot small pellets.

No one had bothered to tell Thompson about the Turkish guard that had been killed there days before or about the town's hair-trigger mentality. Thompson did notice that after he did his handgun joke, the Canadian and Turkish commanders, sitting in the front row, were immediately hustled out of the ballroom.

The rest of the variety show was an abysmal failure. After it was over, Thompson learned not only the recent history in Cyprus but also how close he'd come to being killed. The Turkish commander had been allowed bodyguards for the performance. When Thompson brought out his little BB gun, seven Turkish body-guards, none of whom spoke English, had instantly stood up in the darkened room and cocked their guns and aimed them at Thompson.

Thompson learned one other little detail, after the fact. The

Turkish bodyguards tended to shoot first and ask questions later, because, according to their law, if the commander died under their protection, they all had to die as well.

In an unlikely location, René Lemieux learned that a performer can get a standing ovation for the simplest of acts.

Lemieux was part of a children's theater company that toured a version of *Gulliver's Travels* all over the world. He played the part of Gulliver as a clown.

When the troupe was booked for Russia, the director suggested that Lemieux, who delivered four monologues, learn them in Russian. So he studied with a dialect coach and learned the new language phonetically.

When the show was performed in Russia, the audience was very appreciative that Lemieux had learned some of the dialogue in their native tongue, for most of the audience did not know French. Dozens of bouquets of flowers were given to them after the show.

Since they were next bound for the Republic of Georgia, a former part of the Soviet Union, a Georgian translator Lemieux met in Russia had a new idea: Why not learn the last speech in Georgian? There was a section of that final monologue in which Gulliver spoke of his great sadness about living in this world. It had always moved Lemieux. He agreed.

But he only had two days to learn Georgian, which is as different from Russian as French is from Italian. For the next two days, everywhere Lemieux went, on buses, in restaurants, hotels, museums, the Georgian translator worked with him as he memorized the final speech in Georgian.

In Georgia, the theater they performed in had three balconies and held four thousand people. When he reached the final monologue, switching from French, Lemieux began to speak in Georgian.

He had barely said a sentence when four thousand people stood as one, applauding, cheering, waving, crying. It was a reaction, based on a simple decision, that was unlike any audience response Lemieux ever had or was likely to have ever again.

Actress Heather Summerhayes was in the audience to support her friend Peter Dvorsky when he was in *Born Yesterday* at Toronto's St. Lawrence Centre. But Dvorsky's performance was overshadowed by an unexpected performer on the stage whose history had nothing to do with the Garson Kanin play.

At the beginning of the second act, Jimmy Blendick came on and delivered a short monologue as he paced back and forth. Suddenly a man jumped up from behind a sofa at the center of the stage. He wasn't an actor.

"You can't see me!" he shouted, incorrectly.

Blendick came to a dead stop and the man repeated himself. "You can't see me!"

Blendick could see him all right, and so could Summerhayes and the rest of the house, collectively holding their breath, wondering how this intruder had gotten onstage.

"What the hell are you doing?" Blendick demanded. "We're trying to do a play here."

"You can't see me!" the obviously bonkers man said again and began prancing around on the stage.

Blendick turned toward the audience and asked for a stage manager to help.

Then Dvorsky entered the scene and, unlike everyone else in the St. Lawrence Centre, he really had not seen the man. He certainly did now, though, and he watched the man skip around on the set like a child on a playground. Dvorsky and Blendick looked at each other, at the man gallivanting about, and then again at each other. Blendick shrugged and, as if communicating in code, they both began to chase after the head case. A stage manager joined them and the man was finally captured and taken off.

The audience had been too fascinated by this bizarre scene to laugh, but when Blendick and Dvorsky finally had the stage to themselves, it took them three tries, interrupted by nervous giggling from the crowd, before they could see their way back into the play.

The man who arguably created Theater of the Absurd had his premiere performance interrupted after the first word was spoken onstage.

Alfred Jarry's *Ubu Roi* clearly was not going to coincide with the tastes of the Parisian theatergoers of 1896. The play was about a cowardly, cruel, stupid, childish, vulgar, and generally repugnant man whose quick rise and fall was inspired by Jarry's revulsion for a pompous physics teacher he'd had.

Jarry, who had plastered Paris with handbills about *Ubu Roi*, had assembled the cream of the Paris theater community at the Théâtre Nouveau on December 11, 1896, but they had no idea what they were about to see. After Jarry's own curtain speech, delivered in a nervous and intentionally mechanical mode, the respected actor

Fermin Gémier, on loan from the Comédie Française, strode to center stage as Father Ubu. He wore a huge, padded costume, in the shape of a pear with concentric circles, making him look like an over-weight walking bull's-eye. Mother Ubu, played by Louise France, looked like the female half of a psychotic Punch-and-Judy show.

It was clear from these characters that the audience was not in for an evening of Racine or Molière, but it was the first word out of the mouth of Father Ubu that created an instant riot.

"*Merde,*" Father Ubu said in a metallic voice not unlike Jarry's. Translated, the word was, approximately, "Shit."

The actors were unable to say another word for fifteen minutes. Such an obscenity had never been said aloud in a modern French theater, and some audience members instantly stormed up the aisles and out of the theater. Among the screaming patrons, flailing arms and balled fists could be seen in the first few rows.

Supporters of Jarry's experimental theater shouted back at those who objected. "You wouldn't have understood Shakespeare or Wagner either!" was the cry.

Some who objected to Jarry and this assertion called back, some-what hypocritically, "Shit!"

Gémier, worried that the play might end after only one word of dialogue, improvised a little jig onstage and threw himself across the prompter's box, managing to gain the roiling audience's attention.

He proceeded with the play's next line. Unfortunately, it was another "Shit!"

Again, the house exploded in shouting. Eventually, the players continued through to completion, as Ma and Pa Ubu invaded Poland, did away with civil liberties, murdered anyone who objected, stole from national coffers, and finally, faced with real warfare, showed themselves to be inept cowards.

Ubu Roi had one other performance at the Théâtre Nouveau. It was, alas, a little too nouveau for its time.

The play, the seminal work of absurdist theater, was not performed again until 1908, one year after Jarry, consumed with poverty and the abuse of alcohol and ether, had died.

Critics are entitled to utterly dislike a theatrical production and even to roundly criticize it. But it would seem only fair that they see the entire show before doing so.

The New York critic Kelcey Allen, of *Women's Wear Daily*, a curious publication for theatrical reviews, was in the reprehensible habit of falling asleep in the theater but still reviewing the play he had only partly seen.

One evening, Allen was at a Broadway show and began to snore.

Columnist Walter Winchell, nearby, whispered to his companion, "I see that Kelcey's writing his review early."

The Queen Elizabeth Theatre in Vancouver is a large complex with multiple theaters sharing the same backstage area. It is not unusual for performers to take a few minutes during their intervals to walk down a hallway and watch another production from the wings.

But when actor Nicola Cavendish and a designer friend of hers decided to do just that, they made an accidental guest appearance on the biggest stage in town.

Cavendish was playing a nurse in Peter Shaffer's *Equus* and one night when she had a twenty-minute break, she and Phillip

Clarkson walked down to the backstage door for the large theater where the Royal Winnipeg Ballet was premiering *The Bare Stage*, featuring the voice of Paul Scofield.

As they quietly entered, Cavendish and Clarkson found that the curtain was down, separating them from the audience. It was apparently intermission. Clarkson, a tall, elfin man with a shock of red hair, and Cavendish, in her all-white nurse uniform and cap, decided to wait a few minutes before heading back to *Equus*.

Then, suddenly, the curtain rose, a powerful spotlight shone, and Cavendish and Clarkson were caught onstage, a fifty-foot shadow of themselves cast on the wall behind them.

The commanding voice of Paul Scofield was heard, declaring the beauty of the bare stage.

Not on that night, it wasn't.

Cavendish and Clarkson realized, too late, that they had ventured onstage just before the beginning of the show and they remained stock-still as the ballet came out and began performing in front of a sold-out house, dancing around them as if they were part of the scene.

When another curtain came down, they made a hasty exit.

The next day, Cavendish was walking down Granville Street when she crossed paths with theater critic Colin Thomas.

"Nicky!" he called out in a friendly manner. "Caught your performance with the Royal Winnipeg Ballet last night. Loved it!"

Dennis Christopher was starring with Farrah Fawcett in a production of *Butterflies Are Free* by Leonard Gershe. In the Burt Reynolds Theatre in Jupiter, Florida, Christopher played a blind man. One night, he would wish to be both blind and deaf.

This sensitive love story was disrupted by an obese woman in the front row of the dinner theater making nasty comments and, inexplicably, bird calls. Then she lifted up her dress, exposing herself to the performers.

Christopher's body spasmed after witnessing this, even though his character was supposed to be blind.

The extremely fat and bizarre woman's behavior had a far-reaching effect on the audience as well. One man, upon witnessing a flash of her pulchritude, vomited at his table. This prompted a couple of other patrons to faint dead away.

While there is a plethora of stories about things going wrong and bringing shows to a crashing halt, one particular night in the theater, everything went magically right, and the audience would not let the actors leave.

The Broadway opening of *Mister Roberts* at the Alvin Theatre on February 18, 1948, turned into a run of 1,157 performances over three years. The play, written by Joshua Logan and Thomas Heggen, based on Heggen's novel, was set on a U.S. Navy cargo ship in the Pacific during World War II. But the opening night performance was not just a success artistically and critically. The audience response afterward was tumultuous. Curtain call after curtain call brought the actors back. Marlene Dietrich was spotted in the audience, standing on her chair, screaming and clapping.

Finally, Henry Fonda, playing Roberts, stepped forward to speak and the tumult died down.

"That's all that Josh Logan wrote for us, but if you really want us to, we'll do it all over again."

Mister Roberts was named Best Play in a brand-new awards ceremony that was presented the following year. Named after tireless theater advocate Antoinette Perry, it was called the Tony Awards.

The actress Olive Logan published a book in 1870 entitled *Before the Footlights and Behind the Scenes* detailing the commitment and attention American audiences paid to live theater in the latter part of the nineteenth century.

One such example was a production of Dickens's *Oliver Twist* given in Lowell, Massachusetts. When the curtain came down on the play, the audiences, reluctant to leave the theater, remained in their seats.

After a few minutes, with minimal movement in the house, a stage manager came forth in front of the curtain and made the following proclamation:

"Ladies and gentlemen, I wish to inform you that the play has terminated. As all the principal characters are dead, it cannot, of course, go on."

Playwrights Howard Lindsay and Russel Crouse, at the apex of their success, began to produce theater. Joseph Kesselring's *Arsenic and Old Lace* was one such venture. In fact, they took Kesselring's thriller manuscript, turned it into an outlandish comedy, and changed the title, which was originally *Bodies in Our Cellar.*

Despite their revisions, Lindsay and Crouse did display a real care for their producing duties. They often followed productions on the road, listening carefully to the delivery of the actors to note any places where built-in laughs were not being achieved.

Crouse followed *Arsenic and Old Lace* to Pittsburgh. He sat in the back of the house one night jotting down notes throughout the show.

When the lights came on for the intermission, a woman in the audience berated Crouse, assuming he would rather write than pay attention to a major visiting production.

"What's the matter with you?" the woman angrily demanded. "You haven't laughed once tonight. You're one of the reasons Pittsburgh doesn't get more good productions!"

Producer-director-actor Henry Miller had great success with the play *The Great Divide* by William Vaughn Moody; it played on Broadway for two seasons. The real divide was, once again, in Pittsburgh, where it had been critically panned during its pre-Broadway run.

But after a nice run at the Princess Theatre from 1906-07, Miller decided to forgive Pittsburgh. Pittsburgh, however, had not forgiven Miller.

In the middle of a love scene with actress Margaret Anglin, Miller sensed customers leaving the theater. He stopped performing and stomped angrily to the front of the stage.

"Get back to your seats!" he screamed at the scurrying crowd. "You have already insulted me once, the last time I played this oversized smudge pot, and I won't let you do it again!"

Some of the patrons, overwhelmed by Miller's intensity, went back to their seats. However, a few moments later, others began to leave, and this set Miller off once again.

"Knaves and varlets!" he shrieked.

Anglin grabbed his sleeve. "Stop being a jackass, Henry," she said. "The theater is on fire."

John Barrymore showed greatness in his career as an actor, but one area in which he fell woefully short was patience with audiences.

When Tolstoy's *Redemption* was staged at the Plymouth Theatre in 1918, Barrymore was angered by the insistent coughing coming from the audience one night. During intermission, he employed someone to buy him a sea bass of considerable size.

Rather than taking it home for dinner, Barrymore secreted it inside his coat when he went onstage for the second act.

As soon as the first round of coughing was heard, Barrymore, with a flourish, produced the large fish and tossed it into the first few rows of the house.

"There," he yelled, "busy yourselves with that, you damned walruses, while we proceed with the play!"

It is rare to hear someone boo a performance. It is rarer still to hear such a thing on Broadway. Add a production directed by John Gielgud, starring the likes of Richard Burton, Hume Cronyn, and others. Now, imagine the person booing no fewer than six times during a generally impressive production.

Hamlet has, at this point, been produced more than sixty times on the Great White Way. Only once did a rude patron ruin its production. On May 6, 1964, a member of the audience at the Lunt-Fontanne booed six different times, during both quiet soliloquies and Burton's curtain speech at the end.

The aforementioned speech by Burton, after the repeated disruptions, went this way:

"We have been playing this production in public for over eighty performances. Some have liked it. Some have not. But I can assure you, we have never before been booed."

His speech was well received.

Except for one person, who booed again.

The ramifications of this performance are worth noting. Burton returned to the Regency Hotel, where he and his new wife, Elizabeth Taylor, were occupying an entire floor. Burton relayed the story of the one patron who could not be pleased. Taylor, who had not done live theater at that point, showed little sympathy for her husband and watched television while he spoke.

After trying to impress upon Taylor the significance of such an affront, with no result, Burton lost his temper and kicked in the screen of the television.

The next performance of *Hamlet* featured Burton limping, with a broken foot.

Burton reassured his cast that all would be well, saying, "Some critics have said that I play *Hamlet* like Richard the Third anyway, so what the hell is the difference?"

Amanda Abel is the granddaughter of comedy great Eddie Cantor and, just like dear old Grandpa, she is a performer in the musical theater and sometimes has to be pretty damned quick on her feet, even when she's not dancing.

She was performing with her partner, Michael Taylor Gray, at The Villas in Palm Springs, an outdoor theater surrounding a swimming pool. Most of the audience was gay and very receptive to their humorous song, "All the Good Men Are Gay."

However, one man in the audience wobbled to his feet drunkenly, loudly insisting, "Well, I happen to be straight." The man continued to congratulate himself on being heterosexual and Abel pleasantly congratulated him, too, and then went on to sing the next song, "Class"—something the man clearly could have used.

But the drunken man, insecure about being surrounded by homosexual men, now started approaching the performers, unrestrained by anyone.

He had Abel and Gray cornered near the edge of the pool when Gray, singing the line, "Whatever happened to . . ." then added his own lyric, "SECURITY?"

Abel was again tested when performing solo at the club Monteleone's West in Encino, California. An elderly friend of hers who was struggling with Alzheimer's disease and had become extremely forgetful was in the audience and forgot herself.

Abel was singing the ironically titled, "How Long Has This Been Going On?" when her senior friend began shouting that someone had taken her purse. Abel incorporated her panic into the lyrics:

"I could cry salty tears / When her purse disappears / Can't someone help her, dears / How long has this been going on?"

The audience cheered and a waitress found the purse in the ladies' bathroom, just where the elderly friend had left it.

Kenneth Williams was in the London revue *Share My Lettuce*, which was clearly intended as a silly bit of fun. Early in the run, one boisterous patron apparently did not care for the style. Characters in costumes of various shades came out to talk about their individual colors.

A man came out and announced, "I am pink."

He was greeted by an obnoxious male reply from the stalls: "How dreadfully effeminate."

Williams entered in his costume and delivered the line, "I am green."

The same unpleasant customer spoke out, "Oh, dear, another pansy."

"Be quiet, madam," Williams retorted.

The laughter at the patron's expense sent him angrily scurrying to the box office, requesting a refund. He was refused, with much more politeness than he himself had exhibited.

Anne Nichols was part of a vaudeville duo with her husband, Henry Duffy. Alas, they were so poor, they could not afford to buy comedy sketches from writers for their act.

In desperation to create a career for herself, Nichols wrote a touching melodrama, about Abe Levy and Rosemary Murphy, who keep their interfaith marriage secret from their parents—for a while. Nichols wanted to bring the audience to tears. Instead, during its first presentation, while she was onstage, Nichols was shocked when they laughed continuously.

Back in her dressing room, still stunned by the unexpected

reaction, Nichols got a further surprise: a manager bearing a contract for her writing services.

This led to Nichols producing the play herself. It became one of the longest-running shows in Broadway history.

Abie's Irish Rose ran for more than five years on Broadway and was made into two separate films.

John Brougham was the manager of the Broadway Lyceum Theatre in the mid-nineteenth century and hailed as a theatrical innovator. One of his greatest theatrical bits of direction fooled and fascinated the 1851 crowds that witnessed it.

The play was *A Row at the Lyceum or Green-Room Secrets.* In the greenroom of a theater, actors in their street clothes assembled for the reading of a play within the play. Then an actor, identified as Mrs. B., entered and looked over her part in the play within the play prior to the reading.

But surprisingly, before it could begin, a man clothed in Quaker garb stood up in the middle of the audience and pointed an umbrella at eye level. He slowly left his aisle and made his way toward the stage, saying the actress playing Mrs. B. looked a great deal like someone named Clementina.

As the Quaker gentleman approached the stage, his manner grew more assured and amazed.

"It is. It is my wife. Come off that stage, thou miserable woman!"

The audience members began to take sides with either the Quaker man or the cast of the play. There were shouts of "Shame! Shame!" "Put him out!" and "Sit down!" and "Police!"

The cast grew agitated, and the actress playing Mrs. B. looked like she was going to run offstage in fear. The Quaker man battled his way toward the stage and was intercepted by two uniformed policemen who grabbed him and dragged him up onto the stage.

And then reality descended upon the theatergoers. The cast, including the Quaker man, who was played by Brougham himself, configured themselves in a semicircle and the epilogue was spoken. There was a bit of truth, though, in the theatrical device. Mrs. B. was, in fact, Mrs. B., Brougham's wife.

Audiences were so thrilled to be fooled in this manner, they took their friends to see the show. The secret was well kept and they savored seeing their friends' shocked faces, inside the Lyceum, during the attack of the Quaker. This repeat business guaranteed Brougham's show a long and prosperous life.

Milton Berle was performing at a luncheon for the Banshees in New York. He customarily picked on a cigar smoker and, one night, he found one clouded in smoke.

Berle moved toward the man and readied for the kill.

"Don't you ever inhale?" Berle started in.

But he had picked on a comedic actor named Hugh Herbert.

"Not when you're in the room," Herbert shot back.

Theater criticism is about many things, not the least of which is simply personal taste. After all the names are spelled correctly and the plot is summarized accurately, it is all about difference of opinion. And as with much in the performing arts, there is critical approval and there is popular approval.

Never has a critic, then, been so wrong about the eventual success of a production as the critic who created a disturbance on the opening night of Tom Jones and Harvey Schmidt's musical *The Fantasticks*.

The lighthearted musical about love opened at New York's Sullivan Street Playhouse on May 3, 1960. It closed forty-one years later, having played 17,162 performances. Its run set a record for musicals anywhere in the world and it still stands as the longest-running show in the history of American theater.

It played in every state in the Union—11,103 productions in 2,000 U.S. cities and towns. *The Fantasticks* has been produced more than 700 times in 67 nations, from Afghanistan to Zimbabwe.

Among those stars of the stage who played a part in its phenomenal success were Jerry Orbach, F. Murray Abraham, Liza Minnelli, and Glenn Close.

Tom Jones, who cocreated the phenomenon, was in the wings on opening night, getting ready to make an entrance as a performer, when he heard a commotion.

The aforementioned critic was actually walking across the stage with his girlfriend, trying to leave. There were no side exits in the Sullivan Street Playhouse then, and the critic made the only exit possible, right in front of the performers.

Outside, his girlfriend groused, "What's this thing about?"

In the intimate Bush Theatre in London's Shepherds Bush, Michael O'Hagan was performing in *Belfry*, part of Billy Roche's *The Wexford Trilogy*. He wound up with a most unusual acting partner.

The lights went down in preparation for the beginning of the play. O'Hagan suddenly felt someone rush by him, and he instinctively knew something was wrong.

The lights came up and O'Hagan walked through a door and onto what was usually an empty stage. Only this night, the actor came face-to-face with another man and it was not the actor who shared the stage with him during the play.

The man looked terrified but he could not seem to move, caught in the lights. As it was an Irish play and O'Hagan is definitely Irish, he queried, with a harsh brogue, "What the fuck do you want?"

The man made some sounds, but none of them qualified as words.

"I've asked you the question," said O'Hagan, distressed by this mysterious nonactor. "I won't ask you again."

The man was still unable to move or respond. So O'Hagan covered by saying, "I don't think you should be here." He walked the interloper, who was moving stiffly, to the exit of the theater and pushed him out the door.

O'Hagan's fellow actor then came onstage and the play proceeded.

At the interval, O'Hagan learned his unexpected scene partner was a burglar who had entered the theater by the back stairs, not realizing that when he entered in the dark, he was about to appear in a play. When O'Hagan shoved him outside the theater, the stage manager was waiting for him and he was promptly arrested.

O'Hagan is also responsible for helping convince a fellow actor to get out of the business. Robin Lefevre was with O'Hagan on a seventeen-foot scaffold in *Julius Caesar.* The dead and dying, at the end of the play, are heaped up onstage and Lefevre, as Marc Antony, delivers the famous Shakespearean speech that contains the line, "This was the noblest Roman of them all."

Lefevre somberly looked over the carnage onstage and, holding his emotions in check, he boomed out to a British audience, "This was the hoblest Noman of them all." He paused very briefly and continued with the speech.

But the theoretically dead soldiers, wearing armor, begin to clang and rattle from laughter.

A spotlight hit O'Hagan, who managed to keep a straight face. Then, when the spotlight went out, O'Hagan leaned over to the actor who, as Octavius Caesar, had the final speech.

"Follow *that*," O'Hagan whispered.

The light came up on the actor, who could not speak because he was laughing all over again.

After about seventeen seconds of corpsing and no dialogue, the stage manager figured it was a wash and ordered a blackout.

Lefevre came offstage and told O'Hagan and others, "I can't take this. I'm never going to act again." He didn't. O'Hagan did him a favor. Instead, Lefevre is now an accomplished director on Broadway and in London.

Jack Gilford recounted a whale of a tale about a major mix-up that forced an audience member to "face the music."

In the 1950s, there was a summer tour of the musical *Finian's Rainbow*, by E. Y. Harburg, Fred Saidy, and Burton Lane. Gilford and Edie Adams were starring in the tour, which found itself at the Westbury Music Fair on Long Island.

There is a character in the musical named Senator Billboard Rawkins who is racially prejudiced against black people and is punished by Og the leprechaun. His punishment? Rawkins is turned into a black gospel singer.

When *Finian's Rainbow* was performed on Broadway, the budget was sufficient to hire two different actors to portray Rawkins, one white and one black. Such was not the case during the tour. As the theater was in the round, the producer had a crew in the aisle who would change the costume for the actor playing Rawkins. Also, black makeup was applied to his face and, in about forty-five seconds, the actor would run back up the aisle and onto the stage as a gospel singer.

On opening night at the Westbury Music Fair, the cast had one cue-to-cue rehearsal. They were told that it would be completely dark inside when the lights went out. This was the case during the moment Rawkins was to change skin color.

The actor playing Rawkins unfortunately ran down the wrong aisle, finding no crew. Simultaneously, a member of the audience chose that exact moment to make a dash down his aisle to go to the bathroom. The patron ran into the arms of a waiting crew, who started taking off his clothes and putting on a new costume and black makeup all over his face.

Though the patron tried to protest, he was overwhelmed by the anxious crew rushing to make their deadline. "Shh! We don't have time!"

When the lights came up, the audience member, now a black gospel singer in appearance, called out helplessly, "Alice? Alice?"

In 1967, the Canadian government, celebrating the centennial of the country, decided to present a production of the comedy of manners *Charley's Aunt* as a gift to the Inuit people living in the tundra.

Bruce Gray was one of the actors who had only one week of rehearsals before being flown out, with a stage manager, to Sudbury, in the north of Ontario. From there, they took a bus over paved roads, then "corduroy roads" (made of logs), and for the last quarter mile, by Ski-Doos, or motorized sleds. It was August and there was sixteen inches of snow.

After two days of travel, they reached the tiny village of Gogama and the community center where they were to perform *Charley's Aunt* that night. The stage was one-quarter the size of the stage on which they had rehearsed. The set was instantly reduced to two chairs and a table.

The cast had no time to re-block their movements, for the Gogama Ladies Auxiliary took them off to a dinner of overcooked vegetables and an unidentifiable form of meat. Thirty minutes before the performance, the cast returned to the community center to see about two hundred Inuit Indians arrive. Not one of them had ever seen a play before.

At eight o'clock, the traditional hour for theater to begin, the lights dimmed, in the time-honored way, just before the action began.

But the Inuit in Gogama had their own traditions, and when the lights went out, shouts were heard and chairs were overturned. The Indians ran outside.

How could they possibly object to the play before the action had even started? Gray and the others learned the reason for the violent reaction after the wife of the local chieftain explained it to the stage manager.

Many of the Inuit in that remote community were engaged in adulterous affairs with others. Since most of the Indians carried knives, many of them feared being stabbed in the dark as revenge for their infidelities. So advised, the stage manager dimmed the lights only slightly, so that audience members could keep a wary eye on each other, and the play began again.

There were no other overreactions for the first act of the play. Unfortunately, there were no reactions whatsoever. The audience expressed nothing. Performing an Edwardian-era farce with no laughter from the audience made the actors' jobs rather daunting.

The cast insisted that the stage manager go onstage at intermission and encourage the Inuit to laugh at the actors. There was an argument as to whether an audience can be forced to find something funny if they don't find it funny. The actors prevailed.

The stage manager addressed the Inuit Indians, trying to explain the humor that was totally alien to their culture.

"See," the stage manager insisted at one point to the blank faces before him, "it's really funny when the man dresses up in a woman's clothes!"

Some of the Indians nodded that they'd understood, and others made sounds of comprehension. The second act began. Gray came onstage with the opening line, "Hello, Charley."

The audience exploded in laughter.

They laughed uproariously at virtually every line uttered in the second act, again throwing the actors off.

When the second act was completed, the cast sent the stage manager out again to explain, with some reticence, how to be an audience. The stage manager expressed their appreciation for all the laughter but tried to explain that not every line can be interpreted as being hysterically funny.

Again, the tribe members nodded affirmatively and made clear they understood.

Act 3 got under way, and the Inuit were now beginning to follow the intricacies of the plot. The laughter stopped entirely, but they now whispered to each other, explaining, questioning, and commenting on the farcical storyline of *Charley's Aunt.*

When the play ended, there was complete and utter silence. The cast took their curtain call. There was not a sound in the Gogama Community Center. But the audience was not leaving, either.

The chieftain summoned the cast to come out again. Gray and company did so, and the chieftain addressed them.

"There is no sin worse than for a man to betray his manhood," the chieftain explained angrily. "It is not right for a man to dress like a woman."

"Especially for love," added the chieftain's dour wife.

The cast and stage manager suddenly realized that, according to the culture of the Inuit, *Charley's Aunt* was not a comedy. It was a tragedy about a person loving someone so much, he betrayed his own dignity by dressing in a woman's clothes.

The Inuit demanded to know why the actors treated so terrible a subject so lightly.

The actors had no answer to give, and the Inuit stood up and left.

Gray and his fellow theater brethren stared out at a sea of overturned chairs and listened to the sounds of Ski-Doos noisily starting up and driving off, into the summer snow of a land that had tried and failed to understand the strange magic of their theater.

ACKNOWLEDGMENTS

MANY THANKS TO those who provided research help: Amanda Abel, Shari Albert, Tony Alicata, Woodie Anderson, R. S. Bailey, Jordan Baker, Raven Bast, Peter Bliznick, Steve Bluestein, Amy Brenneman, Randy Brenner, Hindi Brooks, Carrie Brown and Michael Grossberg at the *Columbus Dispatch,* Stacy Burris, Jeremy Caplan at *Time* magazine, Linda Castro, Maria Ciaccia, Kevin Collins, Doug Cooney, Bart DeLorenzo, Merle Debusky, Kevin Doyle, Elizabeth DuVall, Nicola Elson, Beth Falcone, Steve Feinberg, Julian Fellowes, Lissa Ferreira, David Figlioli, Ian Flanders, David Gaines, John Gallogly, Janet Gari, C. J. Gelfand, Joe Gilford, S. E. Gontarski at Florida State University, Bruce Gray, Bob Gutowski, Meredith Hagedorn, Jean Haggard, Larry Dean Harris, Ron Harris, Judd Hollander, Dr. Diane Howard, Christine Howey, Suzy Hunt, Tom Jacobson, Jim Jansen, Jenifour Jones, S. Marc Jordan, Corinne Kason, Reed Kalisher, Gerry Katzman, David Kaufman, Leigh Kennicott, Terry Kingsley-Smith, Miles Krueger, Karen Kondazian, Richard Kramer, Gary Klavans, Cathy Ladman, Jeffrey Landman, Darrell Larson, Terry Lee, Mark Harvey Levine, Simon Levy, Hal Luftig, Cindy Lu, Al Marill, Garry and Lori

Marshall, Melanie McPherson, Sal Mistretta, Kris Montgomery, Steve Moore, Barbara Musgrave, Richard Nathan, Daniel Noah, Liam O'Brien, Kathi O'Donohue, Michael O'Hagan, Jackie O'Keefe, Laurel Ollstein, Tony Pasqualini, Melinda Peterson, Phil Proctor, Bill Rauch, Ronnie Rohrback, Mjka Scott, Richmond Shepard, Todd Shotz, Willard Simms, Carrie Snow, Richard Stein, Andrea Tate, Byron Tidwell, Toni Tomei, Janet Waldo Lee, Elyzabeth Gregory Wilder, Richard Alan Woody.

And personal thanks to:

My publisher, John Oakes; my agent, Bob Diforio; and Bruce Bauman, Denise Fondo, Peter Hay, Simon Levy, James Robert Parish, Carrie Snow, Allan Taylor, Nancy Weems, and especially Jofie Ferrari-Adler, who first said yes to this project and made my dream, and all these people's theatrical nightmares, come back to life.

INDEX

INDEX

INDEX

INDEX

STOP THE SHOW!

CPSIA information can be obtained
at www.ICGtesting.com
Printed in the USA
BVHW01s1510030118
504050BV00001BA/1/P